Better Homes and Gardens®

EASY CRAFTS TO MAKE TOGETHER

750 FAMILY-FUN IDEAS

Meredith® Books • Des Moines, Iowa

EASY CRAFTS TO MAKE TOGETHER

Editor: Carol Field Dahlstrom
Writer: Susan M. Banker
Designer: Angie Haupert Hoogensen
Copy Chief: Terri Fredrickson
Publishing Operations Manager:
   Karen Schirm
Edit and Design Production Coordinator:
   Mary Lee Gavin
Book Production Managers: Pam Kvitne,
   Marjorie J. Schenkelberg, Rick von Holdt,
   Mark Weaver
Contributing Technical Assistant: Judy Bailey
Contributing Copy Editor: Arianna McKinney
Contributing Proofreaders: Callie Dunbar,
   Karen Grossman, Sara Henderson
Technical Illustrator: Chris Neubauer Graphics, Inc.
Editorial Assistants: Cheryl Eckert, Kairee Windsor

Meredith® Books
Editor in Chief: Linda Raglan Cunningham
Design Director: Matt Strelecki
Managing Editor: Gregory H. Kayko
Executive Editor: Jennifer Dorland Darling

Publisher: James D. Blume
Executive Director, Marketing: Jeffrey Myers
Executive Director, New Business Development: Todd M. Davis
Executive Director, Sales: Ken Zagor
Director, Operations: George A. Susral
Director, Production: Douglas M. Johnston
Business Director: Jim Leonard

Vice President and General Manager: Douglas J. Guendel

Better Homes and Gardens® **Magazine**
Editor in Chief: Karol DeWulf Nickell

Meredith Publishing Group
President: Jack Griffin
Senior Vice President: Bob Mate

Meredith Corporation
Chairman and Chief Executive Officer: William T. Kerr
President and Chief Operating Officer: Stephen M. Lacy

In Memoriam: E.T. Meredith III (1933–2003)

All of us at Meredith® Books are dedicated to providing you with information and ideas to create beautiful and useful projects. We welcome your comments and suggestions. Write to us at: Meredith Books, Crafts Editorial Department, 1716 Locust Street—LN112, Des Moines, IA 50309-3023.

If you would like to purchase any of our crafts, cooking, gardening, home improvement, or home decorating and design books, check wherever quality books are sold. Or visit us at: bhgbooks.com

Cover Photograph: Andy Lyons

Time Together

It's always fun to "make things." The very process of using simple materials to create a craft or decorative project that looks great is a special feeling in itself. But "making things" together is more than twice the fun. It's not just the process and the wonderful product anymore—now it is time together. During the process of creating that clever project together gives you time to talk about most anything.

While you are cutting the colorful paper to make a placemat, you might be visiting about last night's ballet lesson. While you are gluing the pretty flower motifs on the front of pinwheels you might be discussing why that once best friend doesn't seem so friendly anymore. While you are creating a bird feeder from grapevines, you might just find out who is the very best soccer player.

Creating crafts together is so much fun. But spending time with the ones you love is what it is really all about.

Enjoy!

Carol Field Dahlstrom

Contents

CHAPTER 3

Feel-Good Gifts

Join family talents to craft awesome gifts to please everyone on your gift list.

CHAPTER 4

Fun to Wear

No need for cookie-cutter looks; work together to create cool fashions.

CHAPTER 7

Handcrafted Parties

Whip up your own party essentials and let the fun begin.

CHAPTER 8

Out and About

Make family travels even more memorable with projects all mapped out to help.

5 Top Family

Kids love to put their imaginations and creativity to work crafting. And if you're right there at the table with them, that's a bonus! Here are five tips to help your family get the most out of your crafting time together:

1 MAKE TIME

Within each busy week, make sure you carve out time for crafting with your kids. They will look forward to it and you might be surprised at all the cool stuff you can make together. It's a great way to fuel their creativity and spark wonderful conversation.

2 BE PREPARED

While many of the projects in this book use special supplies, you'll find several common items for many of the crafts. Items to keep on hand are
- a variety of glues for different surfaces, such as paper, glass, wood, fabric, and plastic
- pencils and marking pens
- scissors, including decorative-edge
- a ruler
- a variety of papers, including tracing and decorative
- newspapers (for keeping the table clean!)
- artist's smocks (to keep the kids' clothes clean!) For instructions to make the smock shown, *left*, turn to *pages 8–9*.

3 KEEP ORGANIZED

Whether you have a crafting room or gather at the kitchen table, organize your supplies in clear, stackable containers. Place a label sticker on one end of each container and mark it neatly. Using stickers allows

Bright Idea
······

Let each of the kids make a crafting wish list and then pick up the supplies when you see them on sale.

Crafting Tips

you to change the label easily should you wish to fill the container with something different.

When you use up a supply, write it on an ongoing crafts shopping list. Keeping items on hand will save you time and frustration when creative urges strike.

4 TIDY UP TOGETHER

Remind the kids that once the craft is completed, the pickup process is a group effort. Adhering to this routine will add to every family member's crafting enjoyment.

5 KEEP THE IDEAS GOING

Along with crafting the oodles of nifty projects in this book, take your kids to crafts shows, art galleries, and crafter's studios. It's a great way to support and encourage their artistic skills and personal expression.

Great satisfaction awaits as you sit down with your kids to craft. You'll find you grow even closer as you make things together. And that's what being a family is all about—spending time with one another and enjoying every minute of it.

Talk With Your Kids
Research and study famous artists together.

Little Picasso Smock

Here's a quick way to turn a pillowcase into an artist's smock.

SUPPLIES
Pillowcase; scissors; iron
Tracing paper; pencil
Straight pins; sewing machine
Thread; rickrack in jumbo
  and narrow widths; buttons
32 inches of narrow twill
  tape, ribbon, or cording
Two ½-inch Velcro circles
Ruler

WHAT TO DO

1 Cut both sides of the pillowcase open and press out wrinkles. Trace the pattern, *below*, onto tracing paper; cut out. Place pillowcase flat and pin the neck opening pattern to the center, lining up the fold line to the center seam of the case. Cut out the neck.

2 Turn under the raw edge along each side; hem on the machine. Turn the raw edge around the neck to the outside; stitch. Pin jumbo rickrack around the neck; stitch in place, overlapping the rickrack ends on the back of the opening. Trim the smock with rickrack and buttons as desired.

3 Cut the twill tape into four 8-inch pieces. On the inside of the smock, pin the end of one of the pieces to the shoulder seam 2 inches in from neck opening and stitch in place. Repeat for the other shoulder seam. Turn smock right side out and stitch the remaining two pieces of twill tape over the same spot, turning the raw ends under before stitching. For each shoulder, tie the two pieces of twill tape together, gathering up the excess fabric at the shoulder.

4 Along one side measure 18 inches up from bottom edge and stitch each section of the Velcro circle to front and back panel. Repeat for other side. Hand-sew decorative buttons over the front circle if desired.

Center Front

Fold

Neck Opening Pattern

Cool for School

From playful lunch boxes to superneat locker accessories, discover oodles of great projects to make together as you get ready for fun at school.

Silly Circus Lunch Boxes

Happy-Go-Lucky Clown

SUPPLIES

Crafts foam in pink, green, and bright pink; scissors
Rectangular white lunch box with top-lift lid (available at crafts stores)
Strong glue, such as E6000; 1-inch pom-poms in purple, yellow, royal blue, green, turquoise, and bright pink
Three 1½-inch red pom-poms
Black permanent marking pen

Bright Idea
·····
Pack your kid's lunch box with a surprise! Use circus-theme cookie cutters to trim sandwiches in entertaining shapes.

12

DRESS UP FOAM SHAPES WITH BRIGHT POM-POMS
TO BLANKET A PLAIN LUNCH BOX WITH PIZZAZZ.

Talk With Your Kids
Make a list of movies that have a lion in them.

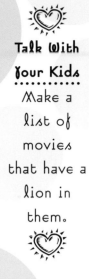

WHAT TO DO

1 From pink foam cut a circle approximately 4 inches in diameter. From green foam cut a triangle for hat. From bright pink cut two circular cheeks about 1½ inches in diameter. Glue the foam shapes to the front of the lunch box.

2 Border the hat with purple, yellow, royal blue, and green pom-poms. Glue a turquoise pom-pom to the tip of the hat. Glue a bright pink pom-pom collar around the bottom of the face, a large red pom-pom nose in the center, large red pom-pom hair at the sides, and alternating turquoise and royal blue pom-poms around the lid. Let the glue dry.

3 Use a permanent marking pen to draw face details, swirls, and "No Clownin' Around...Let's Eat!" in various areas of the lunch box.

The Friendly Lion

SUPPLIES

*Pencil; round white lunch box with side-lift lid
 (available at crafts stores)*
Crafts foam in yellow and black; scissors
Strong glue, such as E6000
1- and 1½-inch pom-poms in yellow and orange
Black permanent marking pen

WHAT TO DO

1 Trace around the lunch box lid on yellow foam. Cut out the shape. Cut two triangular yellow ears and one black nose. Glue the foam pieces in place on the desired side of the lunch box.

2 Border the face with alternating yellow and orange pom-poms, placing the larger pom-poms at the sides. Let the glue dry.

3 Use a permanent marking pen to make face details, zigzags, lines, and "I'm as hungry as a lion!" in various areas of the lunch box.

13

Page Parkers

MAKE PLAYFUL BOOKMARKS TO HOLD YOUR SPOT.

Picture-Perfect Bookmarks

SUPPLIES

*Photos; sharp scissors; ruler; pencil; assorted print and card stock papers
(3 to 4 sheets for each bookmark); glue stick; double-sided tape*
*Assorted stickers; confetti fillers (purchased confetti or decorative
punches and paper to make your own); buttons*
Clear Mylar polyester film; tape; decorative-edge scissors (optional)
Hole punch; ribbon or assorted beads strung onto thin wire

WHAT TO DO

1 Cut out an image from the photo with scissors. Measure and cut out
the background paper, allowing plenty of room for the image. Using a
glue stick or double-sided tape, adhere the photo onto the card stock.
(The card stock used, *below*, measure about 2½×7½ inches.)

2 Using the glue stick,
adhere the matted photo
onto a piece of card stock.
Cut around the bookmark,
leaving a narrow margin.

3 Decorate the bookmark
with stickers, confetti
fillers, and buttons. If you
like, use decorative
punches and paper to
create loose confetti for
filling the bookmark.

4 Cut a piece of polyester
film 2 inches longer and
2 inches wider than the
bookmark. Cut a 1-inch
square in each corner. Fold
the top and bottom edges
and then the sides around
the bookmark. Tape the
polyester film to the back of the bookmark along the
top, bottom, and one long side. Slip confetti fillers
into the bookmark. Tape the open side closed.

5 Using double-sided tape, adhere the bookmark to a piece of card stock and cut out again, leaving a narrow margin all around. If you like, use decorative-edge scissors to cut along side border.

6 Punch a hole in the last paper layer and insert a length of ribbon or wired beads.

I-Love-to-Read Kite Bookmark

SUPPLIES

Tracing paper; pencil; scissors
Gold paper with blue dots; card stock in orange,
  blue, and purple
Glue stick or double-sided tape; ⅝-inch-wide star punch
Alphabet beads; ⅜-inch-wide star beads
Tapestry needle
14-inch length of ⅛-inch-wide orange satin ribbon
Pinking shears

WHAT TO DO

1 Trace the pattern, *below*, onto tracing paper. Cut out the pattern. Draw one pattern on the gold paper and one on the orange card stock. Cut out both kites. Cut the orange kite into quarters. Referring to the photo, *right,* glue or tape two of the quarters to the gold kite. Punch out two blue stars and glue them to the orange sections.

2 Plan the beaded message, placing a star bead between each word. Thread the tapestry needle with ribbon. String the beads onto the ribbon from the beginning of the message. Return the ribbon back through the message starting at the second to last bead. Glue or tape the ends of the ribbon to the back of the kite.

3 Glue or tape the kite to a large piece of purple card stock. Cut out, leaving a narrow margin. Repeat with blue card stock, using pinking shears to cut out the shape.

continued on page 16

**I-Love-to-Read
Kite Bookmark
Pattern**

Talk With Your Kids
Share stories with each other and encourage your kids to write their own books.

Page Parkers continued
Pet Pals Bookmarks

Bright Idea
Frame a series of animal bookmarks for a child's room.

SUPPLIES
Ruler; pencil; scissors
Card stock in blue, orange, yellow, white, and pink; tracing paper
Hole punches in $1/16$-, $1/8$-, $3/16$-, $3/8$-, and $1/2$-inch diameters
Glue stick; black fine-tip permanent marking pen
Yellow mini brads (available in scrapbook stores)

WHAT TO DO

1 For each body, measure and cut out a $2^1/4 \times 6^1/2$-inch rectangle from card stock. Round the corners.

2 Trace the desired patterns, *opposite*, onto tracing paper and cut them out. Cut the pattern pieces from card stock in a color that contrasts with the body. Punch tiny holes at the Xs shown on the patterns using the $1/16$-inch hole punch.

3 Punch circles for the eyes and irises from card stock using various hole punches.

4 Referring to the photos, glue the eyes to the body. Glue the nose in place. Draw facial details with the black marking pen.

5 Attach the ears and tail to the body using the yellow mini brads.

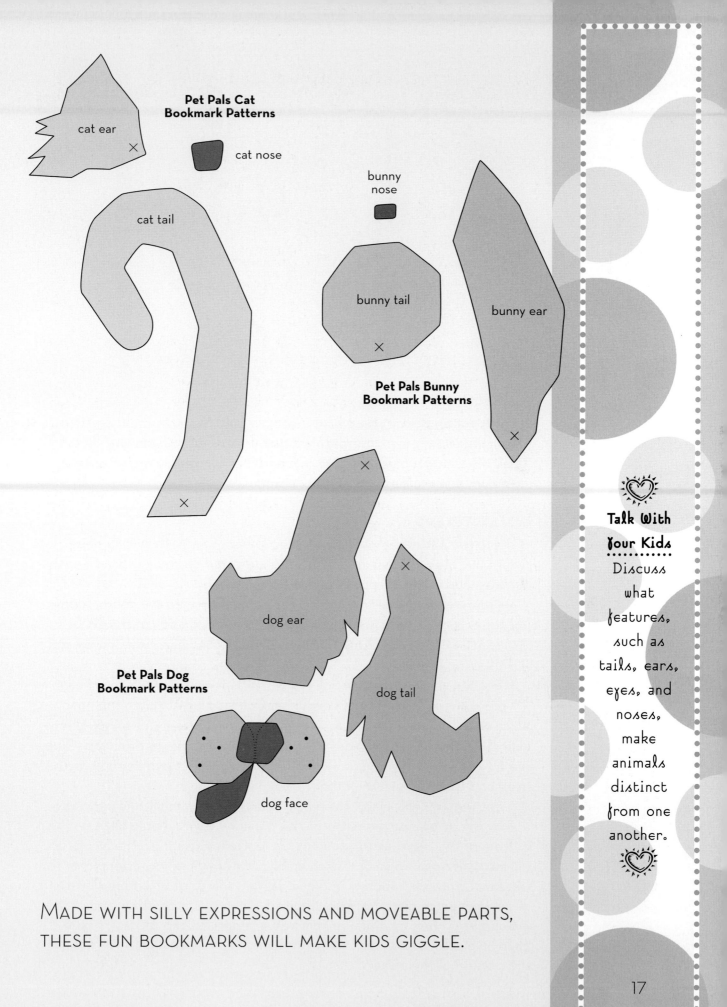

Pet Pals Cat Bookmark Patterns

cat ear

cat nose

cat tail

bunny nose

bunny tail

bunny ear

Pet Pals Bunny Bookmark Patterns

dog ear

dog tail

Pet Pals Dog Bookmark Patterns

dog face

Talk With Your Kids

Discuss what features, such as tails, ears, eyes, and noses, make animals distinct from one another.

MADE WITH SILLY EXPRESSIONS AND MOVEABLE PARTS, THESE FUN BOOKMARKS WILL MAKE KIDS GIGGLE.

Just-for-Fun Pencil Toppers

SUPPLIES

Tracing paper; pencil; scissors; ¼-inch hole punch; crafts knife; crafts foam in yellow, green, purple, blue, and orange; pencil; pinking shears Thick white crafts glue; hot-glue gun and glue sticks; 2⅜-inch-diameter red pom-poms; yellow star button; orange chenille stem; ruler

WHAT TO DO

1 Trace the patterns (enlarging as noted), *opposite*, onto tracing paper. Cut out the patterns. Punch holes as indicated on the patterns. For the airplane, also cut out the slits with a crafts knife.

2 Draw around the patterns on crafts foam, referring to the photos, *above*, for colors. Cut out the shapes, punch the holes, and cut the slits.

3 For the flower, push the pencil tip through the hole in the leaves and then the flowers.

4 For the snake, cut stripes of yellow crafts foam using pinking shears. Glue the strips to the front and back of the snake. Match the head piece to the head of the snake, aligning the holes. Use a dot of hot glue near the holes to secure the head. Glue pom-pom eyes to the head. Glue the tongue inside the mouth. Punch the pencil tip through the hole in the head and then through the other holes in the body.

5 For the airplane, insert the wings through opposite slits as indicated by the arrows on the pattern. The punched holes should align on the bottom of the plane. Hot-glue along the bottom edge. Push the airplane tail into the remaining slot. Punch eight circles from yellow crafts foam for windows. Glue the windows in place. Thread the star button onto one end of a 5-inch piece of orange chenille stem. Then push the other end of the chenille stem through the tiny hole in the propeller. Slip the end of the chenille stem into the front of the airplane. Push a pencil into the hole in the bottom of the plane.

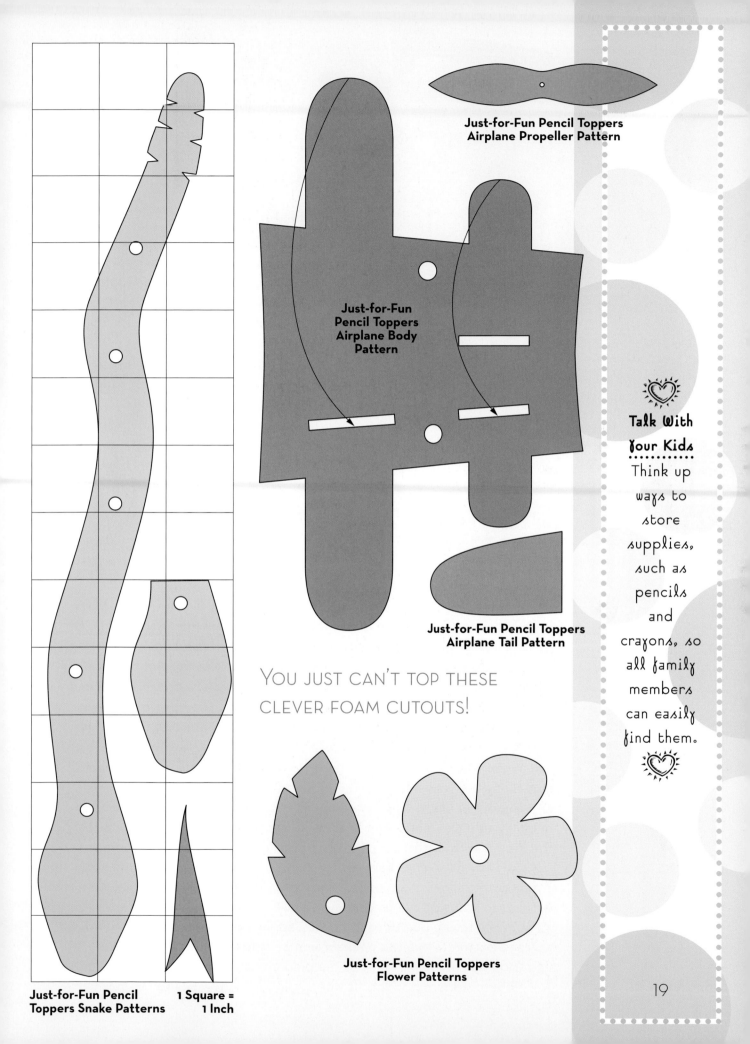

**Just-for-Fun Pencil Toppers
Airplane Propeller Pattern**

**Just-for-Fun
Pencil Toppers
Airplane Body
Pattern**

**Just-for-Fun Pencil Toppers
Airplane Tail Pattern**

YOU JUST CAN'T TOP THESE
CLEVER FOAM CUTOUTS!

**Just-for-Fun Pencil Toppers
Flower Patterns**

**Just-for-Fun Pencil
Toppers Snake Patterns**

**1 Square =
1 Inch**

**Talk With
Your Kids**
Think up
ways to
store
supplies,
such as
pencils
and
crayons, so
all family
members
can easily
find them.

CUT THE BEST PARTS FROM OLD BLUE JEANS AND PUT THEM TO NEW USE ON A HARDWORKING BINDER.

SUPPLIES

Seam ripper; worn pair of jeans
Scissors; ruler
Sewing needle and thread (optional)
3-ring binder; thick white crafts glue
Spring-style clothespins
Appliqués, such as butterflies
 and flowers
1 yard of ⅛-inch-wide green satin
 ribbon; artificial leaves

In-jean-ious Binder

WHAT TO DO

1 Use a seam ripper to remove the pockets and waistband from the jeans. Cut the waistband strip 2 inches longer than the side of the binder. If necessary, sew the loops to the waistband. Cut the inseam on both legs to create a piece of flat fabric; cut two rectangles that measure 3 inches wider and 3 inches longer than the front of the binder.

2 Starting at one edge, spread glue evenly over one-third of the binder front. Center one fabric rectangle over the binder and smooth it over the glue. Continue gluing fabric on the binder until the front is covered.

3 Apply glue to the side of the binder. Smooth the fabric over the edges. Apply a line of glue to the wrong side of the fabric extending beyond the binder front. Fold the fabric under ½ inch along all three edges. Spread glue along the inside edge of the binder. Turn under the 1-inch margins and smooth in place. Use the points of scissors to push the hemmed margin under the metal strip that holds the paper. Secure the fabric to the binder with clothespins; let dry. Repeat Steps 2 and 3 for the back.

4 Spread glue on the spine of the binder. Smooth the waistband strip in place, allowing a 1-inch overlap at the top and bottom. Fold the excess fabric inside the binder and secure with glue.

5 On the wrong side of each pocket, apply a line of glue along the edges and bottom. Place the pockets side by side on the binder front.

6 Glue butterfly appliqués to the binder front. Cut stems from green ribbon. Adhere ribbons, flower appliqués, and leaves to the front.

Bright Idea
· · · · · ·
Shop thrift stores to find used denim.

20

Fun Fleece Tote

SUPPLIES

Graph paper; pencil; scissors; 1 yard of polar fleece; ruler
Fourteen ⁷⁄₈-inch-diameter wood beads
Thick white crafts glue; thread; sewing needle

WHAT TO DO

1 Referring to the diagram, *below*, draw the outline for the back pattern on graph paper and mark the straight grain arrow. Cut out the pattern, leaving fringe areas uncut. Repeat for front pattern.

2 Place the patterns with the arrows on the straight grain of the polar fleece. Cut out. Cut a 3½-inch strip to the desired length for the handle and five ½×10-inch strips to tie the beads to the handle.

3 Place the bag front on top of the bag back. Tie the bottom row of fringe. Gently tie the side fringe, starting at the bottom and working to the top.

4 Turn flap down; slip a bead over the end of the alternating strips of flap fringe. Dab glue inside each bead to hold it in place.

5 Fold the strap in half lengthwise. Mark five points, evenly spaced, along the strap for beads, one at each end with three more points evenly spaced in between. Make a cut at each point. Thread a 10-inch fleece strip halfway through each bead. Pull the ends of the strip through a strap slit and tie in a knot for the three center beads only.

6 Make a small slit in the back at each X on the diagram. Pull the ends of the fleece strips for the end beads through these slits. Tie the ends in a knot inside the bag. Hand-sew across the strap just above each end bead.

THE FRINGED LOOK OF THE '60S IS BACK IN THIS UPDATED TOO-COOL SCHOOLBAG.

Schoolbag Diagrams

19"

11"

7"

11"

4"

FRONT

4"

9"

Front Flap

BACK

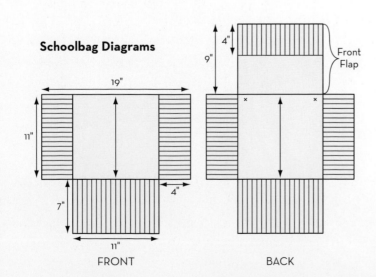

Pasta Pencil Holder

TWISTY, CURVY, AND WAVY NOODLES COVER ANY BOX WITH BUMPY TEXTURE. APPLY STROKES OF PAINT, AND PRESTO—ANY ORDINARY CONTAINER BECOMES A COOL PLACE TO STASH YOUR STUFF!

SUPPLIES

Container, such as a small oatmeal cylinder
Acrylic paints in white, blue, green, yellow, orange, pink, and purple; paintbrush
Pasta in a bunch of different shapes
Thick white crafts glue
Disposable plate

WHAT TO DO

1 Choose a container that is clean and dry. Paint the container white or another solid color. Let it dry.

2 To cover the container, first sort the pasta as shown in Photo A, *above right*. Glue pasta in rows, as shown in Photo B, to create patterns around the container. Or make objects, such as the flower on the lid, *opposite*. Put a large dot of glue onto a plate and let it thicken. Dip each piece of pasta into glue and stick it on the side of the container. Let dry.

3 Squeeze paints on a disposable plate as shown in Photo C. Paint the covered container white. Let it dry. Paint sections using different colors as shown in Photo D. Let dry.

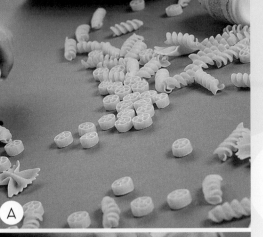

A

B

C

D

Talk With Your Kids
Teach kids how to cook pasta so they can help you out in the kitchen.

23

Desk Smarts

SUPPLIES

*Unfinished wood pieces:
 2 magazine holders, a 6-drawer
 storage chest, a picture frame,
 and a lidded box*
Fine sandpaper
Tack cloth
Flat paintbrush
*Acrylic paints in lime green
 and blue*
Disposable plate
*Wood-handled rubber stamps
 with circle and square designs*
Paper towels
Satin varnish
Drill (for storage chest only)
*Six drawer knobs (for storage
 chest only)*
Bright green gift wrap with a matte finish (for book cover only)
Transparent tape (for book cover only)

KEEP YOUR DESK TIDY WITH THIS HANDY AND BRIGHT ACCESSORY SET.

WHAT TO DO

1 For all wood pieces lightly sand any rough surfaces. Remove the sawdust with a tack cloth.

2 Paint the surfaces, referring to the photos for color suggestions.

3 Decorate the projects with rubber stamps. Referring to the General Stamping Instructions, *below*, apply paint to the stamps and stamp the designs on the wood pieces.

4 Protect each project with two or three coats of varnish. Allow the varnish to dry thoroughly between coats.

5 For the storage chest, drill a hole in the center of each drawer front. Screw on the drawer knobs.

6 For the book cover, cut out a piece of green gift wrap larger than the book. Referring to the General Stamping Instructions, stamp two or more circle designs on the paper. Allow the paint to dry.

7 Wrap the paper around the book and secure it on the inside with transparent tape.

GENERAL STAMPING INSTRUCTIONS

1 Pour a small amount of paint onto the disposable plate. Dip a flat edge of a wedge sponge into the paint. Tap the excess paint back onto the disposable plate.

2 Pat the paint onto the raised design of the rubber stamp. Avoid getting paint in the crevices. Stamp the surface.

3 Repeat the process of applying paint to the stamp for each impression. Clean the rubber stamp periodically with a damp paper towel to eliminate paint buildup on the stamp.

4 After stamping the design, allow the paint to dry.

Talk With Your Kids

Discuss all the different jobs you've had and what ones you liked the best.

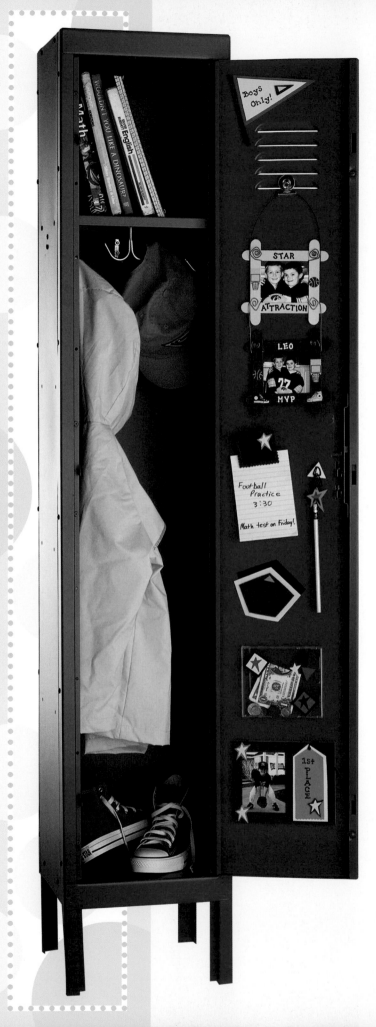

Rockin' Lockers

"Whatta Ya Say?" Signs

SUPPLIES

Tracing paper; pencil; scissors; thick crafts foam in yellow, blue, and green Cling vinyl in green, yellow, and black Foam glue, such as Hold the Foam Alphabet stickers

WHAT TO DO

1 Use a pencil to trace the pentagon and triangle patterns, *pages 29–30,* onto the tracing paper. Cut out the patterns.

2 For the pennant sign, cut a small triangle pattern from the yellow foam, a large triangle from the green vinyl, and a strip from the blue foam. Glue the blue strip to the short edge of the green triangle. Glue the yellow triangle to the green triangle. Cut a tiny triangle pattern from yellow vinyl for a decorative trim; glue it to the blue foam. Cut out the shape, leaving a border all around; glue it to the pennant. Remove the backing from the green vinyl and press the pennant to locker door. Press on alphabet stickers.

3 For the pentagon sign, cut one small pentagon from the blue foam. Cut one large pentagon each from yellow and black vinyl. Glue the blue pentagon to the yellow pentagon. Remove the backing from the yellow shape; press it to the black pentagon. Refer to the photos, *left* and *page 30,* for placement. Adhere alphabet stickers and a green foam triangle at the top of the blue pentagon. Remove backing from the black pentagon; press the sign to the locker door.

DRESS UP YOUR
LOCKER TO FIT YOUR
STYLIN' ATTITUDE.

"Stack 'em" Photo Frames

SUPPLIES
8 jumbo crafts sticks; paintbrush
Acrylic paints in yellow and blue
Thick white crafts glue
Assorted stickers; scissors; ruler
Crafts wire in purple and copper
Adhesive tape; photos
Magnetic clip

WHAT TO DO

1 Paint four crafts sticks yellow and four blue.

2 Place the yellow sticks in a square shape, crossing them as shown in photo, *right;* glue in place. Repeat for the blue sticks. Decorate the frames with stickers.

3 For a top hanging wire, cut a 26-inch piece of purple wire. Make a coil at each end. Bend wire to form an upside-down U. Referring to the diagram on *page 30,* bend coiled wire around the yellow frame.

4 For side hanging wires, cut copper wire into two 13-inch pieces. Coil each end. Referring to the diagram on *page 30,* wrap wires around frames.

5 Tape photos in place. Hang from a magnetic clip.

continued on page 28

Talk With Your Kids

Talk about each of the kids' classes, teachers, and school chums.

27

Rockin' Lockers continued

"Got Cash?" Container

SUPPLIES

Cling vinyl in yellow, blue, green, and black; 1-inch star punch; scissors
Clear, empty compact disc case; crafts glue, such as Goop
Two ³⁄₄-inch-diameter crafts magnets

WHAT TO DO

1 From vinyls, punch out stars; cut out squares and triangles with scissors. As shown in the photo, *page 27*, layer and glue the shapes on disc case; adhere magnets to the back.

"Make a Note" Notepad Clip

SUPPLIES

Pencil; tracing paper; scissors; crafts foam in blue and green
Cling vinyl in black and yellow; pinking shears; decorative-edge scissors
Foam glue, such as Hold the Foam; 1-inch star punch
1³⁄₄-inch silver magnetic clip; colorful notepad

WHAT TO DO

1 Trace the rectangle patterns on *page 30* onto tracing paper; cut out. Cut a large rectangle from blue foam and a small rectangle from black vinyl. Pink the edges of the blue rectangle. Use decorative-edge scissors to trim the edges of the black rectangle. Glue the shapes together.

2 Punch one star from yellow vinyl; glue it to green foam. Cut out leaving a narrow border. As shown in the photo, *page 27*, glue the star to the rectangle; glue the rectangle to the clip. Attach a notepad.

"Make a Note" Pencil and Holder

SUPPLIES

1-inch star punch; blue cling vinyl; crafts glue, such as Goop
Thick crafts foam sheets in green and yellow; scissors; ruler
Black crafts wire; yellow sparkle pencil
³⁄₄-inch-diameter crafts magnet

WHAT TO DO

1 Punch a star from vinyl; glue it to green foam. Cut out, leaving a narrow border all around.

2 Cut a 19-inch piece of wire. Wrap one wire end around pencil top seven times. Glue wrapped wire to pencil. Thread foam star onto wire. Bend remaining wire into a triangle-shape "coil." Wrap the wire end around the bottom of the wire triangle three times.

3 Cut out a yellow foam triangle; glue to magnet. Cut a 7-inch piece of wire. Fold one end of the wire down 1 inch; twist end to form a loop. Bend remaining wire into a coiled triangle slightly smaller than foam triangle. Glue wire triangle to foam triangle. Bend loop to form a hook. Slip pencil onto the hook.

"Lookin' Good" Photo Frame

SUPPLIES

Tracing paper; pencil; scissors; thick crafts foam in yellow, green, and blue
Hole punch; pinking shears; 1/3 yard of 1/8-inch-wide blue satin ribbon
Foam glue, such as Hold the Foam; crafts foam frame with magnets
1-inch star punch; yellow cling vinyl
Black alphabet stickers; photo

WHAT TO DO

1 Trace frame pattern, *page 30*, onto tracing paper; cut out. From yellow foam, cut one large ribbon. From green foam, cut one small ribbon; punch a hole at the top and trim the bottom edge with pinking shears.

2 Fold the blue satin ribbon in half; thread the fold through the hole in the green foam. Take ends of blue ribbon through the ribbon loop; pull up. Referring to the photo on *page 27*, glue green foam shape to yellow foam shape; glue to the frame.

3 Punch three stars from yellow vinyl; glue to scraps of green and blue foam. Cut out, leaving small borders. Glue stars to frame and foam ribbon. Press stickers in place. Glue photo to frame.

continued on page 30

**Rockin' Lockers
"Whatta Ya Say?" Sign
Patterns**

Rockin' Lockers continued

Rockin' Lockers
"Make a Note of This"
Notepad Clip
Pattern

Rockin' Lockers
"Lookin' Good"
Photo Frame
Pattern

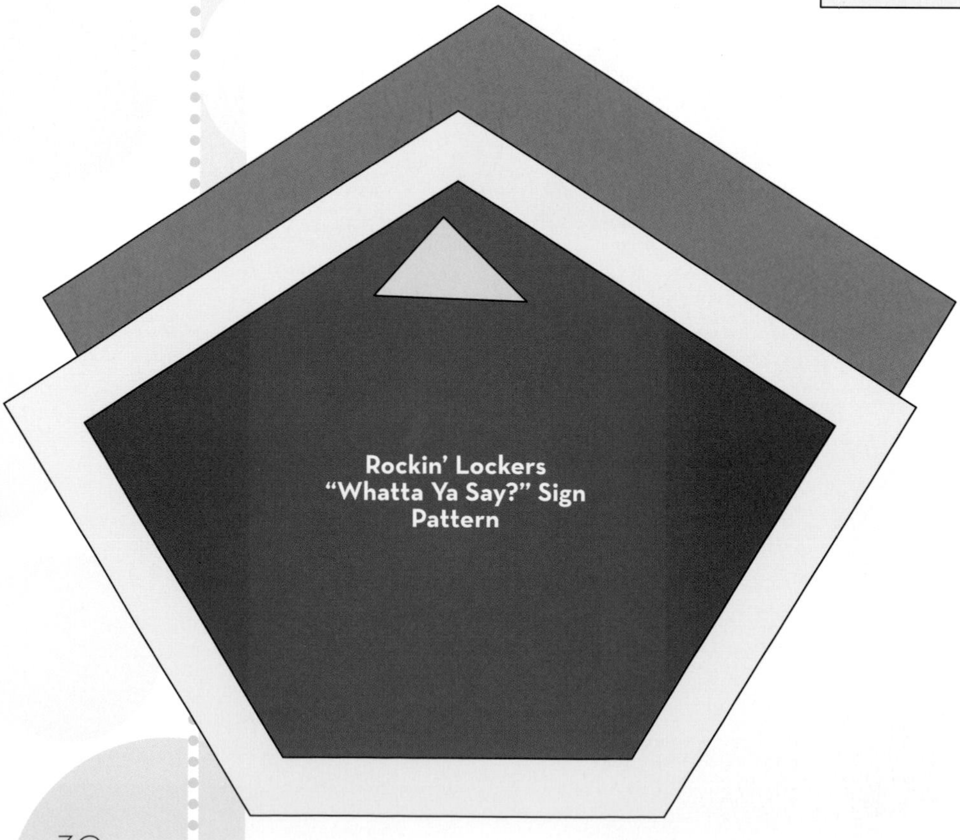

Rockin' Lockers
"Whatta Ya Say?" Sign
Pattern

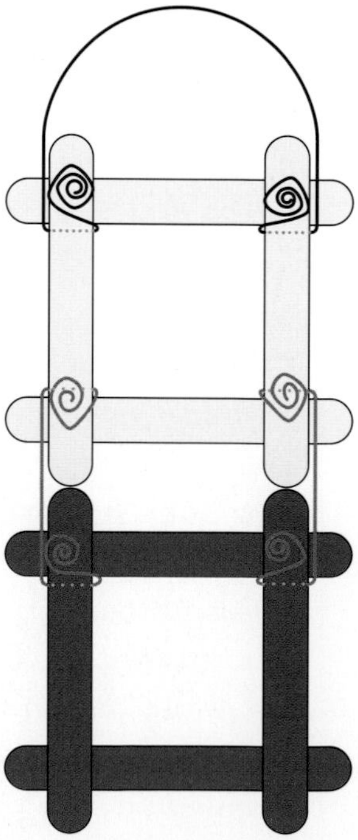

Rockin' Lockers
"Stack 'em" Photo Frames
Wiring Diagram

**Pretty 'n' Pink
"Flower Power" Note Clip
Pattern**

**Pretty 'n' Pink
Glamour Girl Mirror
Flower Pattern**

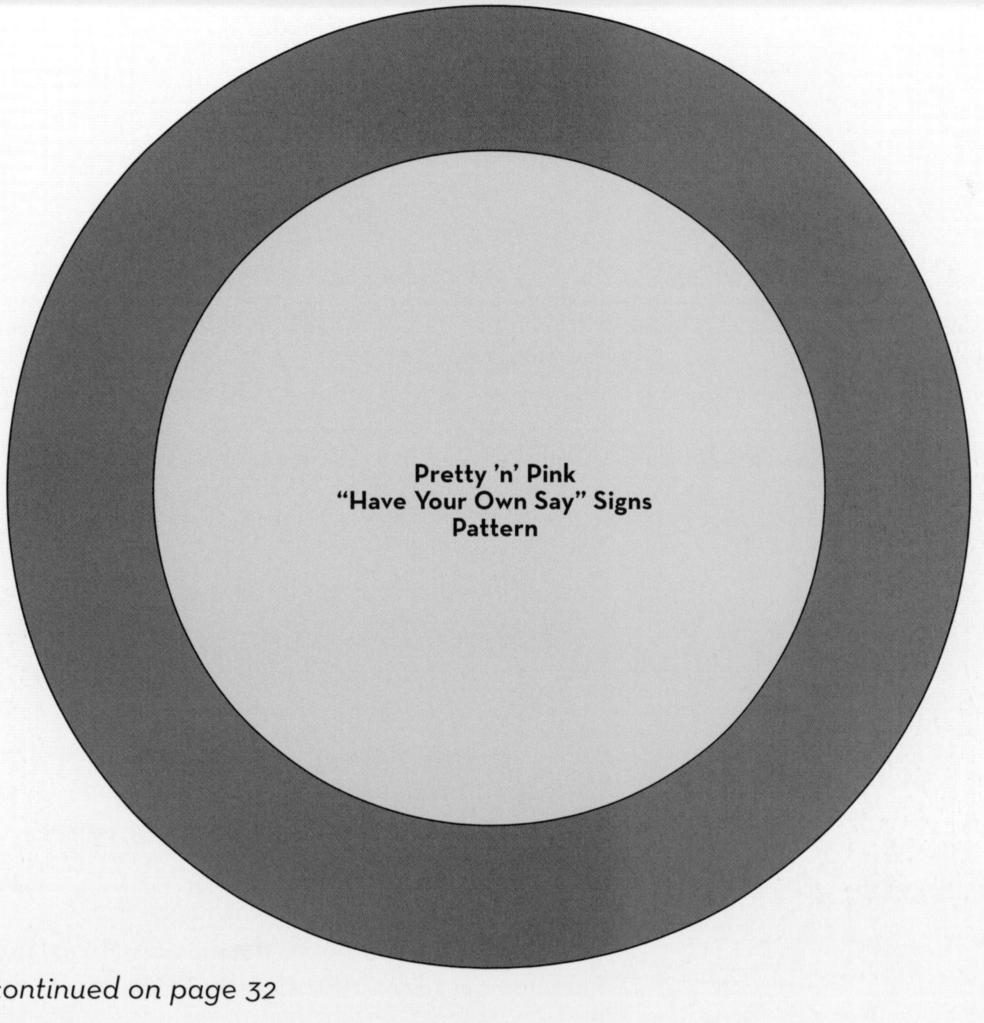

**Pretty 'n' Pink
"Have Your Own Say" Signs
Pattern**

continued on page 32

Talk With Your Kids
Role-play various situations that teach your kids to say "no" when the need arises.

31

Pretty 'n' Pink

"Have Your Own Say" Signs

SUPPLIES

Tracing paper; pencil; scissors; purple cling vinyl; decorative-edge scissors
Lime glimmer felt; thick pink crafts foam
Foam glue, such as Hold the Foam
5/8-inch-wide flower punch
Lime holographic adhesive film
Pink foam flower stickers
Pink acrylic flower jewel
Black alphabet stickers

WHAT TO DO

1 Use a pencil to trace patterns, *pages 31 and 35*, onto tracing paper. Cut out patterns.

2 Trace the large circle and large oval patterns on purple vinyl. Use decorative-edge scissors to cut out the shapes. Cut a small circle from lime felt and an oval from pink foam using decorative-edge scissors. Glue these shapes to the corresponding purple vinyl shapes.

3 For the "Too Cool" sign, cut a large flower from pink foam to fit inside the lime circle. Glue the flower to the lime circle.

4 For the "Girls Rule!" sign, punch out one lime holographic flower and press onto the pink foam flower. Press the foam flower onto the pink foam oval. Glue a pink flower jewel to the center of the foam flower.

5 Spell out phrases with alphabet stickers. Remove the backing from the vinyl and press the signs to locker door.

"Dress It Up!" Locker Fringe

SUPPLIES

Note: *Purchase trims and magnetic tape to fit the width of your locker.*
3-inch-long pink beaded trim
1½-inch-long purple beaded trim
Double-sided tape
Scissors; adhesive magnetic tape

WHAT TO DO

1 Tape the beaded trims together using double-sided tape. Trim the ends even.

2 Peel away the paper from the magnetic tape. Press trim onto the adhesive side. Hang trim in locker.

Glamour Girl Mirror

SUPPLIES

Tracing paper; pencil; scissors
Glimmer felt in purple and lime
Decorative-edge scissors
Sparkle foam flower stickers in lime and pink
Pink foam mirror, such as Foamies, with magnets on the back
Foam glue, such as Hold the Foam
Pink acrylic flower jewels

WHAT TO DO

1 Use a pencil to trace the circle pattern, *page 31*, onto tracing paper. Cut out.

2 Trace three circles on the felt (two on purple, one on lime); cut out using decorative-edge scissors. Press a flower sticker in the center of each circle.

3 Use foam glue to affix the circles to the mirror frame; glue flower jewels in the centers. Let the glue dry.

continued on page 34

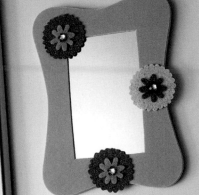

Talk With Your Kids
Discuss ways for your kids to welcome new students into their school.

Pretty 'n' Pink continued

"Best Friend" Photo Frames

SUPPLIES

8 jumbo crafts sticks
Paintbrush; acrylic paints in pink and purple
Thick white crafts glue; white alphabet stickers
Plastic flower trims
Crafts wire in copper and green
Scissors; ruler; photos
Adhesive tape; magnetic clip

WHAT TO DO

1 Follow the directions for the "Stack 'em" Photo Frames on *page 27*.

"Flower Power" Note Clip

SUPPLIES

Tracing paper; pencil; scissors; pink crafts foam
2½ inches of 1½-inch-wide lime beaded trim
Double-sided tape
Lime sparkle foam flower
1- and ⅝-inch-wide flower punches
Purple cling vinyl
Fuchsia holographic foil
Foam glue, such as Hold the Foam
Pink acrylic flower jewels
1¾-inch silver magnetic note clip
Colorful notepad

WHAT TO DO

1 Use a pencil to trace the pattern, *page 31*, onto tracing paper. Cut out the pattern. Trace the pattern on pink foam. Cut out the shape.

2 Affix beaded trim across the bottom edge of the shape using double-sided adhesive tape. Press the lime flower onto the pink foam shape.

3 To decorate the lime flower, punch a 1-inch flower from purple vinyl and a ⅝-inch flower from fuchsia foil. Press the fuchsia flower to the purple flower. Glue a pink jewel to the center. Glue assembled flower to lime flower.

4 Use foam glue to affix the completed pink foam shape to the magnetic note clip. Insert the notepad.

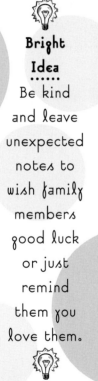

Bright Idea

Be kind and leave unexpected notes to wish family members good luck or just remind them you love them.

"Flower Power" Pencil Holder and Pencil

SUPPLIES

Scissors; crafts wire in lime and purple; ruler; pink pencil
³⁄₈-inch-diameter pink acrylic bead; needle-nose pliers
Crafts glue, such as Goop; lime glimmer felt; bottle cap
³⁄₄-inch-diameter crafts magnet

WHAT TO DO

1 Cut a 19-inch piece of lime wire. Make a tight coil in one end of the wire; begin wrapping the wire around the pencil. Make about seven wraps.

2 With the rest of the lime wire length, form a large coil for the flower center. Thread on a bead at the end of the coil. Using needle-nose pliers, make a tiny loop at the wire end to hold the bead in place.

3 Cut a 24-inch piece of purple wire. Wrap the wire end around the outside coil of the flower center. This is the bottom of the flower.

4 Bend a ³⁄₄-inch-long petal shape in the purple wire; wrap the purple wire once around the outside coil for the flower center. Continue bending and wrapping wire to form five petals. Wrap remaining wire around top of pencil; secure to pencil with glue.

5 For the magnetic hook, cut a 1-inch circle of lime felt using a bottle cap for the pattern. Glue the circle to the magnet. Cut a 7-inch piece of purple wire. Fold one wire end down 1 inch and twist the end to form a loop. Coil the other end of the wire into a circle. Bend loop to form a hook. Glue coiled shape to the lime circle. Hang pencil on hook.

Pretty 'n' Pink
"Have Your Own Say" Signs
Pattern

Talk With Your Kids

Share what your favorite colors are and why. Then let your kids incorporate their favorite colors into their room decor.

36

Dazzling Desk Set

SUPPLIES

Rubbing alcohol and paper towels
Desk set in black or off-white
Acrylic enamel paints in pink, green, blue, and white
Disposable plate; paintbrush

WHAT TO DO

1 Clean the surfaces of the desk set with rubbing alcohol. Let the desk set dry.

2 Put a small amount of each paint color on the plate. Place one or two drops of white into each color without mixing. When using paint, pick up the color and a little white on the paintbrush. Brush once lightly on the plate to slightly blend the colors.

3 Paint simple, playful motifs, such as squares, circles, and stripes, on the black or off-white areas of the desk set. Wash the brush before changing colors. Let the paint dry.

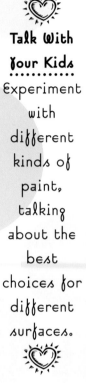

Talk With Your Kids
Experiment with different kinds of paint, talking about the best choices for different surfaces.

THESE PAINT-SPLASHED ACCESSORIES GARNER MILES OF SMILES. CHOOSE BRIGHT COLORS TO LIVEN UP A BLACK DESK SET OR PASTEL SHADES TO ENHANCE OFF-WHITE PIECES.

37

Itty-Bitty Books

WITH THESE
BOOKS, YOU ARE
THE CRAFTER,
AUTHOR, AND
ILLUSTRATOR TOO!

Emma's Secret Journal

SUPPLIES

Ruler; pencil; 6-inch-square spiral notebook; crafts knife; scissors
³/₁₆-inch-wide green ribbon; scrapbook paper in magenta with white dots
Thick white crafts glue; ½ yard of ³/₈-inch-wide magenta satin ribbon
Pinking shears; adhesive-back felt in light blue and magenta
Paper daisies (available in scrapbook stores)

Bright Idea
Be creative! Use buttons, gems, or old earrings for the flower centers.

WHAT TO DO

1 Centered on the first page, draw a 4-inch square. On a protected work surface, cut out the square through all the notebook pages using a ruler and a crafts knife. Tie green ribbon into bows around the cut layers at the top, side, and bottom as shown, *opposite*.

2 Cut scrapbook paper to fit inside the back cover; glue in place. Glue the last page of the tied pages to the back cover.

3 Cut magenta ribbon in half for ties; glue in place inside journal. With pinking shears, cut a square of blue felt and a smaller square of magenta felt; glue on cover. Make flowers from circles of blue felt and scrapbook paper with ribbon stems; glue in place. Center paper daisies on felt flowers.

Kay's Journal

SUPPLIES

Scrapbook papers; composition book
Paper adhesive
12 inches of beaded rickrack
1/8-inch wide pink satin ribbon
Stickers in alphabet and heart shapes
Assorted beads

WHAT TO DO

1 Cut papers to fit the cover. Spread adhesive over the cover and place the papers on top; smooth out any wrinkles. Glue on trim and press stickers onto cover.

2 For the bookmark, knot one end of ribbon; thread with beads. Adhere unknotted end inside front cover.

Books, Books, and More Books

SUPPLIES

Scissors; thick white crafts glue
Assorted scrapbook papers, including white
Fabric scrap; 6×8-inch spiral notebook
Computer
Book clip art, downloaded from
   Internet
1/2-inch-wide ribbon

continued on page 40

books books and more books!

Itty-Bitty Books continued

WHAT TO DO

1 Cut and glue layers of paper and fabric and glue to the notebook front. Using your computer, arrange words and clip art; print out design on white paper. Cut out the design shape; glue to contrasting paper. Cut out shape again, leaving a narrow margin. Glue shape to fabric.

2 Thread ribbon through spiral binding and knot. Create a matching bookmark from the scraps.

My Sketchbook

SUPPLIES

9×12-inch rectangle of lightweight cardboard; glue
Striped paper; 3½×4¾-inch piece of white card stock
4×5-inch piece of black card stock
Adhesive-back silver metal letters
8¾×10¾-inch rectangles of drawing paper
¼-inch-wide ribbon

WHAT TO DO

1 Fold cardboard in half, matching short edges. Cut striped paper and glue to cardboard cover. Draw a picture on white card stock; glue to black card stock. Cut it out again, leaving a margin.

2 Adhere the picture and letters to the front. Fold drawing paper in half to fit inside the cover. Wrap ribbon around the sketchbook center; tie a bow.

Bright Idea
......
Make extra books to use as gifts.

My School Friends

SUPPLIES

Photo
Yellow cloth-cover photo album
Adhesive dots (available in scrapbook stores)
Rubber alphabet stamps
Ink pads in purple, magenta, olive, and teal
Embroidery thread
Assorted buttons

WHAT TO DO

1 Adhere the photo to the front cover using adhesive dots. Stamp letters in assorted colors on the cover.

2 Use thread to tie some buttons together in pairs. Adhere single and paired buttons to the cover with adhesive dots.

Talk With
Your Kids
Talk about
your
favorite
stories of
their baby
years.

All About Jack

SUPPLIES

Foam appliqués and alphabet stickers
Thick white crafts glue
6×8-inch crafts foam mirror; scissors; 1-inch-wide ribbon
7×10-inch spiral notebook; hot-glue gun and glue sticks
Scrapbook papers; white card stock

WHAT TO DO

1 Glue foam appliqués and stickers to mirror. Cut the ribbon in half and glue to notebook for ties.

2 Hot-glue the mirror to the notebook.

3 Cut scrapbook papers to fit notebook pages; glue sheets of card stock to scrapbook papers. Write about yourself or your child on each page. Glue the pages in place.

Bright Barrettes

SUPPLIES

Tracing paper; pencil; scissors; crafts foam in desired colors
Small hole punch; eyelets in circle, flower, or heart shapes; eyelet tool;
  decorative-edge scissors (optional)
Foam glue, such as Hold the Foam
Barrettes with a smooth, wide surface

WHAT TO DO

1 Trace the desired patterns, *opposite*. Cut out the shapes. Trace around
the pattern pieces on crafts foam. Cut out the shapes.

2 Decide where eyelets are desired and mark them with a pencil. Punch
a hole through each mark. If layering foam pieces to be connected by
eyelets, punch the top layer. Layer the pieces and make a mark in the
center of each punched hole. Punch holes in the bottom layers.

3 With layers together, place an eyelet in each hole; secure with the
eyelet tool.

4 Cut additional details with straight-edge or decorative-edge scissors
or make dots using a hole punch. Glue the details on the foam pieces.
Let the glue dry.

5 Glue the foam pieces to the barrettes. Let the glue dry.

**Bright
Idea**
Glue foam
designs to
a pin back
or plain
bangle
bracelet
to make
pretty
jewelry.

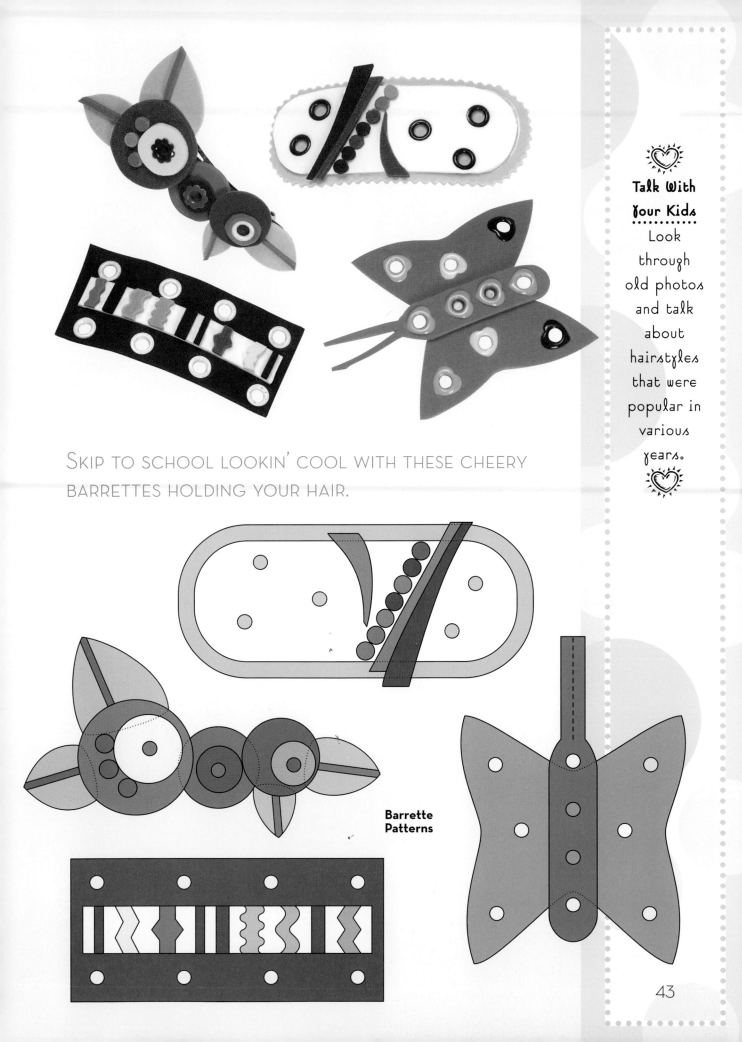

Skip to school lookin' cool with these cheery barrettes holding your hair.

Barrette Patterns

♡ **Talk With Your Kids**

Look through old photos and talk about hairstyles that were popular in various years. ♡

43

Perfect for Pets

Adorable treat jars, endearing framed pictures,
bright sunshiny beds, and more—this chapter is as devoted
to your pets as you are!

Bone China

SUPPLIES
Paint markers
Plastic dinnerware

WHAT TO DO

1 Using a paint marker, write your pet's name on the side of the bowl and your name on a matching cup, plate, and bowl. Write special sentiments about your pet. Include your pet's birthday, a favorite trick, or a funny nickname that you call him. Let the paint dry.

SHOW YOUR PET HOW MUCH YOU LOVE HIM BY CREATING MATCHING BOWLS FOR THE TWO OF YOU.

Pet Place Mats

SUPPLIES
Ruler; pencil; poster board; scissors
Photographs, cutouts, and drawings
Thick white crafts glue
Black permanent marking pen (optional)

WHAT TO DO

1 Measure and mark a 12X18-inch rectangle on poster board. Cut out the shape.

2 Place photographs, cutouts, and drawings on the board. Arrange them as desired and glue all pieces in place.

3 Use the permanent marking pen to write a few words about your pet if you wish.

4 To make the place mats last longer, have them laminated at a photocopy shop.

Talk With Your Kids
Get silly and think up unusual pet names.

Dylan plays with Clara

Maggie hugs Casper

CELEBRATE ANIMALS BY CREATING PET PLACE MATS YOUR FAMILY CAN USE AT THE TABLE. IF YOU DON'T HAVE A PET, CLIP OUT ANIMAL PICTURES FROM MAGAZINES.

47

Paw Print Plaques

💡

Bright Idea
......
Display clay paw print plaques along with your kids' handprint impressions on a plate shelf.

💡

SUPPLIES

Large saucepan
1 cup cornstarch
1-pound box baking soda
1½ cups water
Spoon; cornstarch
Plastic wrap or waxed
  paper
Toothpick; baking sheet
Paint; paintbrush
Tube-style crafts paint

WHAT TO DO

1 In a large saucepan combine 1 cup cornstarch and the baking soda. Stir in 1½ cups water. Cook over low heat, stirring until mixture thickens and forms a ball. Remove from heat.

2 Turn clay out onto a surface dusted lightly with cornstarch. When cool enough to handle, knead the clay until smooth.

3 Cover the clay with plastic wrap or waxed paper; cool completely. If wrapped tightly in plastic wrap, clay can be refrigerated for up to two weeks.

4 To make a plaque, roll a chunk of homemade clay onto a piece of waxed paper. Flatten the clay to be about 1 inch thick Carefully place your pet's paw into the clay until it makes an impression. Scratch your pet's name into the clay with a toothpick.

5 Place clay on a baking sheet and bake in a 300° oven for 30 minutes. Turn off the oven; leave baking sheet in oven 1 hour more. If the clay is still moist, place on a wire rack and air-dry completely before painting. Allow one color to dry before painting with another color. Fill in your pet's name with squeeze-tube crafts paint.

CAPTURE YOUR PET'S PAW PRINTS IN CLAY
TO HANG IN YOUR HOME.

49

Bright Idea
......
Use this technique to design a dish to hold bath toys for kids.

CREATE SOMETHING SPECIAL FOR YOUR BEST ANIMAL FRIEND— A PAINTED FOOD DISH!

Adorable Dish

SUPPLIES

Pet food dish; enamel paints in desired colors
Paintbrushes; alphabet stickers

WHAT TO DO

1 Using the photo for ideas, paint the rim and the side of the dish. To avoid paint getting in your pet's food, leave the inside of the dish unpainted. Paint stripes, flowers, dots, or other small designs. To paint dots, dip the handle of a paintbrush into paint and dot onto the surface. Make flower petals using a small paintbrush. To paint stripes, use a flat paintbrush. Let dry.

2 If you like, outline some of the designs with black paint. Let dry.

3 Adhere alphabet stickers to the side of the dish to spell a name. Press the stickers into place in a straight or wavy line.

Keep-Close Key Chain

SUPPLIES

Black adhesive crafts foam; ruler; scissors
Crafts foam in desired roof color; colorful miniature crafts sticks
Small hole punch; eyelet; eyelet tool
Ball chain key chain; pet's photo; decoupage medium; paintbrush

WHAT TO DO

1 Cut a 1³/₄x3-inch rectangle from black adhesive crafts foam. Trim one short end into a point. From colored foam, cut a triangle slightly larger than the point.

2 Peel off the backing paper from the foam. Starting at the flat, short end, center a crafts stick on the sticky side of the black foam and press in place. Continue arranging crafts sticks side by side until seven sticks are in place.

3 Press the foam triangle on the adhesive point for the roof. Punch a hole ¹/₂ inch from the tip. Push an eyelet into the hole and secure it with an eyelet tool. Thread the ball chain through the eyelet.

4 Cut out your pet's photo in a rectangle small enough to center on the crafts sticks, allowing at least ¹/₂ inch on either side. Round the top of the photo. Use decoupage medium to glue the photo in place. Let the glue dry.

IN MINUTES TURN YOUR PET'S PHOTO INTO A COMPANION KEY CHAIN.

♡
Talk With Your Kids
Develop a family backup plan in case you lock yourself out of the house or the car.
♡

51

EMBELLISH A SEE-THROUGH JAR TO HOLD TREATS FOR YOUR GOOD DOGGIE BOY OR GIRL.

Too-Cute Treat Jars

Good-Dog Canister

SUPPLIES

Ruler; 1-gallon clear plastic jar with lid; tracing paper; pencil
Computer and printer (optional); double-sided tape; bath towel
Black dimensional paint; dog treats; scissors; crafts foam in purple and
pink; dog photo

WHAT TO DO

1 Measure the height and width of the area on the jar to be decorated. (The design *above* covers an 8×12-inch space.) Draw a rectangle with these measurements on tracing paper. Write your pet's name and draw paw prints in the area. Connect the paw prints with a broken line. If desired, use a computer and printer to print your pet's name.

2 Tape the paper inside the jar. To keep the jar from rolling while painting, place a bath towel on

the table. Roll the short ends toward the middle; cradle the jar between the ends. Using dimensional paint, trace the name and design onto the jar. Let dry overnight.

3 Remove the paper from the jar and fill it with dog treats.

4 To make a frame for your pet's photo, cutting a circle of purple foam to fit by the top of the lid. Cut out a smaller circle from the center of this circle, leaving a ½-inch-wide ring. Trim your dog's photo to fit the frame; tape in place. Cut out a pink foam heart and tape it to the rim.

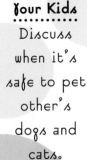

Talk With Your Kids
Discuss when it's safe to pet other's dogs and cats.

Totally Treats Jar

SUPPLIES

Wide-mouth jar with lid
Newspapers
Orange spray paint
Tube-style crafts paints in yellow, light blue, and white
Desired stickers
1-inch-wide wire-edge ribbon
Scissors

WHAT TO DO

1 Wash and dry the jar and lid. In a well-ventilated work area, cover the work surface with newspapers. Spray-paint the lid top and sides; let dry.

2 Use yellow paint to write your pet's name on one side of the jar. Make rings of white and light blue paint dots for flowers. Let dry. Add a dot of yellow in each flower center. Let the paint dry.

3 Embellish the lid and jar with stickers. Tie a ribbon bow around the jar neck. Trim the ribbon ends.

DISPLAY YOUR LOVING PET'S PICTURE IN A LEISURELY, YET PLAYFUL, WINDOW SETTING.

Purrr-fect Picture

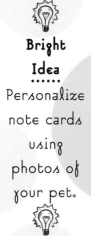

Bright Idea

· · · · ·

Personalize note cards using photos of your pet.

SUPPLIES

5×7-inch whitewashed picture frame
Cloud print paper; scissors; ruler; ivory paper; pencil
Double-sided tape; ¼ yard calico red fabric; iron
Hot-glue gun and glue sticks; yellow wire; yellow flower buttons
Animal picture; adhesive dots, such as Mini Pop Dots

WHAT TO DO

1 Remove glass and frame back from picture frame. Cut a piece of cloud paper to fit inside frame. Measure and cut two long strips of ivory paper (approximately ½ inch wide) to mimic window crossbar. Tape strips of paper together into a crossbar using double-sided tape. Tape crossbar inside frame.

2 Cut two 6×7-inch pieces of calico. Using a dry iron, turn hem under ¼ inch on the two long sides and bottom of each piece. Secure hem to material with double-sided tape. Slightly gather the top of each calico piece with your fingers and hot-glue it to inside of frame.

3 Cut two 3-inch pieces of wire, thread through buttons, and gather calico toward center like curtains. Twist wire to secure. Hot-glue the back of twisted wire to frame and glass edge to frame. Cut your pet from the photo and apply foam mounts to bottom edge of the animal cutout. Adhere cutout to bottom edge of frame.

54

Fancy Fishbowl

SUPPLIES
Fishbowl with 2 flat sides
Glass paints
Disposable plate
Rubber stamp

WHAT TO DO

1 Wash and dry the fishbowl. Avoid touching the areas to be painted. Place a small amount of glass paint on the plate. Spread it around until it is a thin layer.

2 Carefully dip the stamp into the paint. Working on one side of the fishbowl, stamp onto the flat surface. To stamp the rounded sides, carefully rock the stamp back and forth. Change colors as desired, washing the stamp between colors. Allow the paint to dry. Follow manufacturer's instructions for curing the paint.

DISPLAY A PLAYFUL DESIGN ON YOUR FISHIES' HOME SWEET HOME.

Talk With Your Kids
Think up ways to use fishbowls for storage and organization around the house.

55

Pretty Pet Cards

SUPPLIES

Card stock in gold, ivory, and red; scissors; ruler
Animal print papers; glue stick; crafts knife
Animal print ribbon; double-sided tape
Pet photos; tracing paper; pencil
Transparency film, such as Grafix Color Inkjet
Color copier (ink-jet)

WHAT TO DO

1 To make the gold card, measure and cut gold card stock into a 7×10-inch piece. Fold in half. Cut a 4×5-inch rectangle from animal print paper; cut a jagged edge. Glue design to the front of card using glue stick. Cut out a 1³⁄₄×2¹⁄₈-inch center opening in card using a crafts knife on a protected surface. Fold animal print ribbon through center opening of card and secure with double-sided tape on the inside.

USE A TRANSPARENCY OF YOUR PET TO MAKE
A STRIKING CARD FOR SOMEONE YOU LOVE.

2 Lay tracing paper over your pet's photo and trace pet's outline. Trace outline onto gold paper and carefully cut it out using a crafts knife on protected surface. Lay gold outline over pet photo and make an ink-jet color copy of him on transparency film. Let color image dry at least 10 minutes before handling.

3 Cut image out slightly larger than center opening of card and affix to inside of card using double-sided tape. (The image shiny side should be facing out with the rough side of the film inside the card.)

4 Cut a piece of ivory card stock and glue inside the card on the right-hand side as a background to enhance the transparency image.

5 To make the red card, measure and cut red card stock into a 7×10-inch rectangle; fold it in half. Using the photo, *opposite*, as a guide, mark a 2½×4½-inch rectangle and three 1-inch squares on the card front. Cut out the shapes using a crafts knife on a protected surface.

6 Cut pet out of photo using scissors or a crafts knife. Lay cutout on animal print paper and make an ink-jet color copy onto the transparency film. Let color image dry at least 10 minutes before handling. Cut image out slightly larger than the card's openings and affix to inside of card using double-sided tape. (The image's shiny side should be facing out with the rough side of the film inside the card.)

Talk With
Your Kids
Think of people who may need a cheer-up note and then make one and send it to them.

Pet Pillow Pizzazz

SUPPLIES

Tracing paper; pencil
Scissors; felt scraps in turquoise,
  yellow-orange, green, purple,
  orange, and red
Fabric marking pen
Bright pink embroidery floss
Sewing needle; fabric glue
19-inch squares of felt in bright
  pink and yellow-orange
12-inch poly-fil pillow form

GIVE YOUR PET THE ROYAL TREATMENT, BEGINNING WITH A SOFT FELT PILLOW THAT DOUBLES AS A CAN'T-RESIST TOY.

WHAT TO DO

1 Trace the patterns, *below*, onto tracing paper; cut out. Trace and cut four large circles from yellow-orange felt and one from each remaining color. Trace and cut one small circle from yellow-orange felt and two from each remaining color.

2 Layer a small circle on each large one, using the photo, *opposite*, as a guide for color placement. From the top make a small stitch in the center of a group of layered circles and knot the floss on top of the circles. Trim the ends.

3 Glue the red and yellow-orange circles in the center of a 19-inch square of bright pink felt. Glue the layers together. Continue gluing layered circles to the pillow top in three rows. Let dry.

4 Place the decorated pink felt square on the yellow-orange square. Cut $3/4 \times 3$-inch-wide strips along each edge for fringe.

5 Knot the fringe together on three sides of the pillow. To make knots, wrap two corresponding fringe around a finger. Push the ends through the loop and pull snug. Slip the pillow form inside the case and knot the remaining fringe together. *Note:* If the pillow is too plump, make a slit in one side and remove some stuffing before tying the final row of fringe. Stitch the opening closed.

Talk With Your Kids
Be sure your pet is safe by doing an all-family safety check of your home and yard.

Small Circle Pattern

Large Circle Pattern

CHAPTER
3

Feel-Good Gifts

Craft a candle, paint a frame, sculpt some soap—
you'll find more than two dozen great make-it-together
gift ideas.

Bright Idea
⋯⋯⋯
For a child's version of this project, replace the flower with lollipops.

ADORN A FLOWER WITH A LOVELY PAPER ACCENT FOR AN UNFORGETTABLE GIFT.

Romantic Flower Collars

SUPPLIES

Tracing paper; pencil; scissors
Scrapbook papers in floral prints and solids
White paper; 1/8-inch hole punch; glue stick
4-inch-diameter round paper doilies; crafts knife
Needle; white thread; small white crafts pearls

Small and Large Collar Patterns

WHAT TO DO

1. Trace the star patterns, *above*, onto tracing paper; cut out. Trace around the star patterns on assorted floral prints and solids. Cut out a small and large star to make each collar. Punch a hole in the center of each small star.

2. Glue star layers together using a glue stick. Then glue a round doily underneath each star pair. Using a crafts knife on a protected surface, cut a center hole through all three layers. Cut a slit from the center to the edge to allow the collar to slip over the flower stem.

3. Prepare a needle with white thread and sew one white pearl at the end of each star point on each collar. Knot the threads on the underside to secure.

♡
Talk With Your Kids
Explain the difference between annuals and perennials, and talk about what flower scents you like best.

Foam Flower Bouquet

CREATE SPRING-FRESH FLOWERS FROM CRAFTS FOAM TO LAST SEASON AFTER SEASON.

SUPPLIES
Tracing paper; pencil; scissors; decorative-edge scissors (optional)
Crafts foam in desired colors and green; hole punch or awl
Chenille stems in shades of green
Pony beads; foam egg carton

Bright Idea
·····
Use foam flowers to top a wrapped package.

WHAT TO DO

1 Trace the desired flower and leaf patterns on *pages 66–67*. Cut out the shapes.

2 Trace around the pattern shapes on the desired colors of crafts foam; cut out with straight or decorative-edge scissors.

3 Use a hole punch or awl to make a hole near the center of each flower and near one tip of each leaf.

4 Choose two or three chenille pieces for each stem. Twist the chenille stems together until you reach a point where a leaf is desired. Thread a leaf on one chenille stem and secure it with a couple of twists. Place additional leaves in this manner. Slip on the layers for the foam flowers.

5 Slip one, two, or three pony beads on the chenille stems for the flower center. Fold the pipe cleaners around the beads to secure.

6 For the egg carton flower, *above left*, cut out two or three egg cups from the carton. Repeat Steps 3, 4, and 5 to complete the flower.

continued on page 66

Talk With Your Kids

Discuss safe ways to hold a tool, where to store it, and how to protect the work surface.

**Foam Flower Bouquet
Leaf and Flower Patterns**

**Alternate Foam Flower Bouquet
Flower and Leaf Patterns**

Sticker Stationery

Bright Idea
......
To organize stickers and keep them flat, store them in labeled file folders.

SUPPLIES

8½×11-inch sheets of paper in desired colors; scissors
1×3-inch labels in white and green; round stickers in a variety of colors
Marking pens in black and green
Self-adhesive notebook paper reinforcements in desired colors and white

WHAT TO DO FOR THE FENCE STATIONERY

1 Cut three 1×3-inch labels in half along the length of the label to make fence posts. Cut points on one end of five posts as shown in Photo A, *below left.*

2 Stick fence posts on the paper about ¼ inch apart. Arrange fence posts so the points face up and bottom edges are even. Cut the remaining strip in half and press each half across the fence posts as shown in the photo, *opposite.*

3 Position flowers in front of the fence as you wish, using various sizes of round stickers. To make leaves, cut the shape from a large round green sticker as shown in Photo B.

WHAT TO DO FOR THE BUTTERFLY STATIONERY

1 To make the butterfly, cut a round sticker in half. Peel off the backing from half and press it on the paper where you want your butterfly. Peel off the other half of the round sticker and place it next to the first, putting the rounded edges together. Cut a V-shape piece from a sticker for the antennae, adhering small round stickers to each point.

2 Arrange flowers on the bottom of the stationery as you did for the fence stationery. Cut narrow strips from green labels for the stems.

3 Using a marking pen, draw a dotted line below the butterfly as shown in the photograph, *opposite.*

WHAT TO DO FOR THE POLKA-DOT STATIONERY

1 Pick the colors of round stickers and reinforcements you wish to use.

2 Press on the round stickers first, arranging them on the outer edges of the paper. If some extend over the edge of the paper, trim off with scissors.

3 Fill in with reinforcements, pressing some on top of the round stickers; leave a blank space in the middle to write a letter.

A

B

Dear Aunt Jane,
    Thank you
for my new
radio. I love
you!
    Today I

Go sticker
crazy making
this clever
stationery!
Since it's so easy,
make some for
all your friends!

Bright Idea
.....
Another way to recycle old greeting cards: Decoupage them on a hard plastic place mat.

Fancy Knife Fans

LOVE
LOVE
crazy love

SEARCH FLEA MARKETS,
ANTIQUE STORES, AND THRIFT
SHOPS FOR GREETING CARDS
AND BUTTER KNIVES TO MAKE
PRETTY VINTAGE-LOOKING FANS.

SUPPLIES
Greeting cards
Old butter knives, clean and polished
Pencil
Hot-glue gun and glue sticks
Ribbon or silk flower

WHAT TO DO

1 Open greeting card. Place a butter knife inside card, centered on one flap. Use a pencil to draw an outline around the knife. Remove the knife.

2 Apply hot glue within the knife outline. Press the knife firmly onto the glue area as quickly as possible. Place glue on the face of the knife. Close card and press against glue. Tack the card corners together using dots of glue.

3 Tie a bow on the knife handle or glue a silk flower in place. Let the glue dry.

I'M SO LUCKY THAT YOU'RE
My MoM

Talk With
Your Kids
Discuss
ways to say
thanks.

71

Earring Tree

SUPPLIES FOR THE EARRINGS
Thick white crafts glue
Buttons, small appliqués, beads, paper clips, or wiggly eyes
Earring backs; acrylic paint; disposable plate; small ceramic tiles
Pencil with round eraser
Eraser topper in square shape

SUPPLIES FOR THE EARRING HOLDER
Picture frame
Colored plastic canvas
Pencil
Scissors
Thick white crafts glue

Bright Idea
••••••
Make Dad a tie tack holder using a masculine style of frame.

A BLAST TO MAKE, WEAR, AND PUT AWAY—EARRINGS
HAVE NEVER BEEN SO MUCH FUN!

WHAT TO DO FOR THE EARRINGS

1 Glue buttons, appliqués, beads, paper clips, or wiggly eyes to the earring backs using crafts glue as in Photo A, *right*. Allow the earrings to dry thoroughly before wearing.

2 For the tile earrings, put paint on a disposable plate. Dip the round eraser end of the pencil in the paint and dab onto the tile for a flower center. Dip the square eraser topper into the paint to make petals as shown in Photo B. Let the paint dry. Glue an earring back to the tile. Let it dry.

WHAT TO DO FOR THE EARRING HOLDER

1 Take the glass out of the picture frame. Lay the frame on the plastic canvas and draw around the inside of the frame. Use scissors to cut around the shape, as shown in Photo C, leaving about ¼ inch all the way around the shape.

2 Glue the plastic canvas into the back of the frame using crafts glue. Let the glue dry.

3 Insert pierced earring posts through the plastic canvas mesh and attach the earring backs to hold earrings in place.

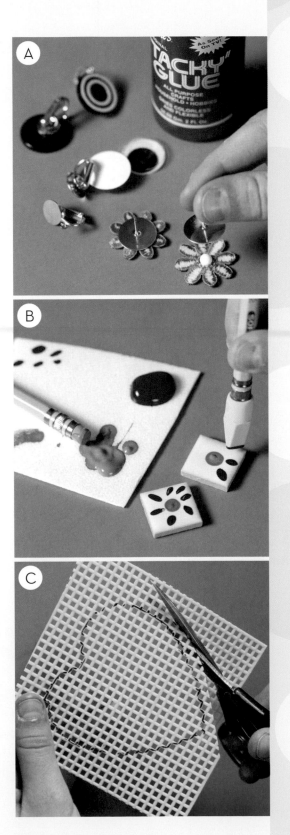

Talk With Your Kids
Talk about why people wear earrings in different countries.

Bright Idea
•••••
For a child's lamp, cover the shade with comic book pages.

Sew-Cool Shade

SUPPLIES

Sewing pattern pieces; scissors; decoupage medium; lamp with white paper shade; paintbrush; rickrack; thick white crafts glue; metal snaps

WHAT TO DO

1 Trim around several pattern pieces. Apply the pattern pieces to the lampshade using decoupage medium. Trim off the overhang.

2 Use decoupage medium to attach rickrack to the edges of the lampshade. Use crafts glue to adhere snaps randomly on the shade. Let dry.

SCOUR THE SEWING ROOM FOR TRIMS AND EXTRA SEWING PATTERNS TO CREATE A LAMPSHADE THAT'S A PERFECT FIT FOR ANY CRAFTING AREA.

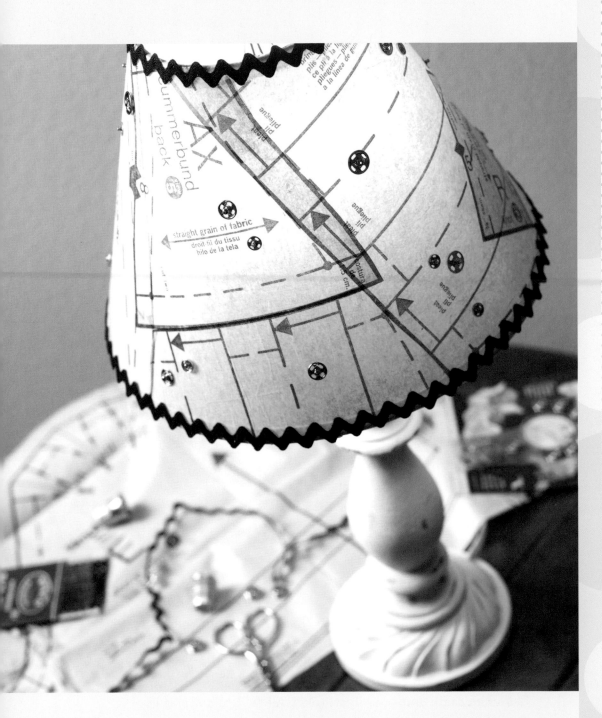

Talk With Your Kids Discuss clothing prices and what you could make to help out the family budget.

Bright Idea

Wrap up pretty soaps with new hand towels for a lovely gift set.

Seashell Soap

SUPPLIES

Blue glycerin soap block; glass measuring cup; knife; white coconut oil soap block Seashells; plastic soap molds

WHAT TO DO

1 Break blue soap block into small pieces. Place in the measuring cup. Carefully slice small bird and sand shapes from the white soap block. Arrange the pieces with seashells in the soap molds as shown, *above.*

2 Melt the blue soap in the microwave following the manufacturer's instructions. Let it cool until a thin film appears on the top of the soap.

3 Skim film aside and pour into molds. Allow it to set and cool completely. Remove soap from molds.

CHERISHED GIFTS ANYTIME OF THE YEAR, SEASCAPE SOAPS BRING BEAUTY TO THE POWDER ROOM.

76

Fancy Flowerpots

MAKE A CHEERY CENTERPIECE THAT IS AS COLORFUL AS A FLOWER FROM THE GARDEN. PEEL-AND-STICK FOAM PIECES MAKE IT EASY TO GROW THESE PRETTY BLOOMS.

SUPPLIES

Terra-cotta flowerpot; dirt; seeds or a small plant
Wide green crafts stick; black permanent marking pen
Adhesive-back crafts foam or crafts sponge flowers and circles

WHAT TO DO

1 Fill the terra-cotta pot with dirt. Plant seeds or a small plant in dirt.

2 Use a marking pen to write your name on the crafts stick, leaving at least 1½ inches blank on each end. Push one end of the stick into the center of the flowerpot.

3 Decide where you want to put foam flowers on the flowerpot. Layer the pieces to make colorful flowers if desired. Peel off the backings and press into place. Press on foam circles if you wish. Make a large foam flower and press it onto the top of the crafts stick.

Talk With Your Kids
Tell them what foods grow well in a garden, then choose one to try.

Butterfly Mugs

SUPPLIES

Solid-color glass coffee mugs
Tracing paper; pencil
Transfer paper
Glass paints in black and other desired colors
Fine-tip and other paintbrushes
Pencil with round eraser

WHAT TO DO

1 Wash and dry each mug. Avoid touching the areas to be painted.

2 Trace the desired patterns, *opposite*. Use transfer paper to transfer the patterns randomly to each mug. To make each butterfly, start with the color portion of the wings. Each wing can be a simple oval or two smaller connected ovals. Use one or two paint colors for each wing. Let the paint dry before making black details.

3 Using a fine-tip paintbrush, paint simple outlines around each butterfly. For each body, paint a small circle for the head with antennae and an elongated oval for the body. Paint dots on the wings and dotted lines below the butterflies if desired. Let dry.

EVERYONE WHO ENJOYS A GOOD CUP OF JAVA LOVES
RECEIVING A SET OF THESE FANCIFUL BUTTERFLY MUGS.
TUCK A COFFEE PACKET OR TWO IN EACH CUP FOR
A WELCOME SURPRISE.

Talk With Your Kids
Explore the world of butterflies together at the library or online.

Butterfly Mug Patterns

4 To make polka dots, dip the eraser of a pencil into paint and carefully dot it onto the surface of the mug, placing dots randomly between butterflies and down the edge of the mug handle. Let dry.

5 If directed by the paint manufacturer, bake the mug in the oven. Let cool.

Bright Idea
......
Use a theme sticker, such as a golf tee or a hammer, and press it on the tie for a tie tack.

Dad's Album

SUPPLIES

Glue stick; two 9⅞×5½-inch pieces of decorative paper for outside cover

Two 6½×4½-inch pieces of mat board for covers

Two 2½×4½-inch pieces of mat board for flaps

Two 8⁵⁄₆×4⅜-inch pieces of decorative paper for inside cover

⅛-inch hole punch

Alphabet stickers

Paper scraps; buttons

1 package of plastic mini pocket album refills
Scissors; large paper clips
15-inch piece of plastic-coated telephone wire; 1-inch-wide rubber band

WHAT TO DO

1 Apply glue to back side of one of the cover papers. Center and lay a cover board and a flap board on paper, leaving a ⅛-inch gap between cover and flap. Fold edges of paper over edges of mat board. Repeat for other cover and flap boards.

2 Center and glue an inside cover paper over each mat board cover and flap. When glue is entirely dry, mark five holes along top edge of cover, ¼ inch down from edge and ¾ inch apart as shown on pattern, *below*. Punch out holes.

3 Decorate the front cover with alphabet stickers or use paper scraps and buttons to make a collar and a tie (enlarge and trace pattern, *below*) for a shirt.

4 Cut binder hole edge off each of the plastic mini pocket album refills. Punch holes across top edge to correspond with holes on mat board covers.

5 Sandwich the album refills between the front and back covers. Use paper clips to hold pieces together. Cut wire into 3-inch pieces. Slip a piece through each set of holes and make a circle about the diameter of a pencil. Twist the ends around each other four or five times. The twisted ends should be on the back side. Cut off excess wire.

6 Fold flaps to outside of each cover and use a rubber band to keep album closed.

7 To stand, remove rubber band from top cover flap only and flip top cover over to back. Overlap the two flaps, slipping the front flap through the rubber band on the back flap.

GIVE DAD A DASHING ALBUM FOR STORING TREASURED PHOTOGRAPHS, NEWSPAPER CLIPPINGS, SMALL WORKS OF ART, AND OTHER CHERISHED KEEPSAKES.

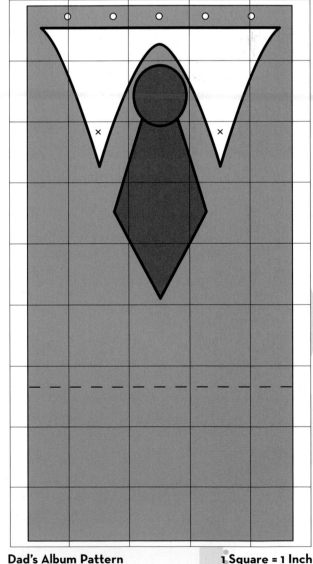

Dad's Album Pattern   **1 Square = 1 Inch**

Talk With Your Kids
Share your ideas about a dream job.

Fairest-of-All
Mirror Set

ANY LITTLE GIRL LOVES TO PRETEND SHE'S A PRINCESS
OR THE QUEEN HERSELF WHEN LOOKING INTO THIS
MAGICAL MIRROR CROWNED WITH SWIRLING COLORS
OF YARN.

SUPPLIES

Thick white crafts glue
Handheld mirror, brush, and comb
  set with smooth, flat surfaces
Paintbrush
Yarns in desired colors
Scissors
Jewels

WHAT TO DO

1 Apply a few dabs of glue on the top of the mirror handle and smear it around with your finger or a paintbrush as in Photo A, *right*.

2 Beginning at the top of the handle, place the yarn on the glue as in Photo B and start winding it around until the entire handle is covered. Apply glue as you go. Choose one color of yarn or several different colors.

3 Cover the back of the mirror with a thin layer of glue and wind the yarn on the glued area. Wind yarn in whatever shape you like as in Photo C. Trim yarn with scissors as needed. Keep changing colors around the shapes until the whole area is covered. Use glue to hold jewels on yarn.

4 Decorate the brush and the comb using the same yarn and jewel techniques.

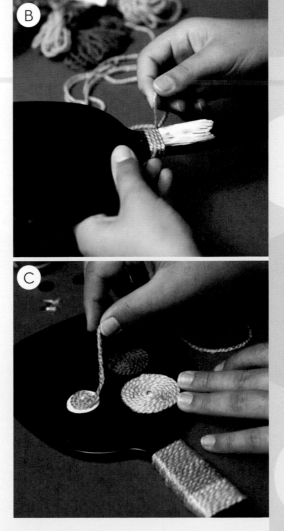

Talk With Your Kids

Discuss how styles have changed since you were their age. Ask them about their favorite fashions.

83

Fingerprint Frame

Bright Idea
......
Make fingerprints to bring charm to plain wrapping paper. Make gift tags too!

LEAVE YOUR MARK ON PICTURE MATS BY MAKING ITTY-BITTY FINGERPRINT BUGS WITH PAINT. STYLIZE LADYBUGS, CATERPILLARS, AND BUTTERFLIES WITH BLACK MARKING PEN DETAILS OR MAKE ANY CREEPY, CRAWLY CRITTERS YOU LIKE!

SUPPLIES

Acrylic paints in bug colors
Frame with double mats
Black fine-tip marking pen

WHAT TO DO

1 To make ladybugs, dip a finger in red paint. Press finger onto one of the photo mats. Make as many red dots as you wish, leaving spaces between the dots. Let the paint dry. Draw spots and curly antennae with a marking pen.

2 To make caterpillars, dip a finger in green paint. Make a bunch of dots in an uneven line. Continue making lines of dots with your finger, leaving space between bugs. Let dry. Make faces and antennae with a marking pen.

3 To make butterflies, dip a finger in any color of paint and make two prints side by side. Continue making butterfly wings like this until you like the way the mat looks. Let dry. Use a marking pen to draw details, such as spots and antennae.

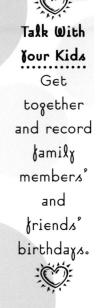

Talk With Your Kids
Get together and record family members' and friends' birthdays.

Tire Tracks Stationery

MAKING NOTEPAPER IS A GAME IN ITSELF WITH THIS SIMPLE STAMP-AND-ROLL TECHNIQUE! FINISH WITH STICKERS RACING ACROSS THE PAGE.

Bright Idea
Use fabric paints to make tire track designs on a pillowcase or a T-shirt.

SUPPLIES

*Miniature toy car with
 treaded wheels*
Black ink pad
Colored papers and envelopes
Truck and car stickers

WHAT TO DO

1 Roll the wheels of the toy car over the ink pad. Next roll them across the papers and envelopes to leave tire tracks. Repeat this as many times as you wish, leaving room to write between the marks.

2 Place truck and car stickers over tracks. Let the ink dry.

Talk With
Your Kids
Discuss
the
importance
of keeping
in touch
with loved
ones who
live far
away.

Embroidered Envelope

PERFECT FOR HOLDING A GIFT CERTIFICATE OR CASH, THIS FLORAL ENVELOPE IS A GIFT IN ITSELF.

Bright Idea
······
Keep felt and embroidery floss on hand for sewing when on car trips. These supplies are inexpensive and easy to organize.

88

SUPPLIES

Tracing paper; pencil; scissors; ruler
Felt in bright pink, white, turquoise, green, purple, and orange
Black embroidery floss; needle; straight pins; scrap paper; hole punch

WHAT TO DO

1 Enlarge and trace the envelope and flower patterns, *below*. Cut out the shapes. Trace around the patterns on the appropriate pieces of felt. Cut out the shapes. Cut a 7½×7¼-inch piece from bright pink felt.

2 Use free-form cross-stitches to adjoin the straight edge of the envelope flap and short edge of the pink rectangle.

3 Using the pattern, *below*, as a guide, pin the large round flower and the leaves in place. Blanket-stitch around each piece to secure them in place. Remove pins. Detail the center of each leaf with running stitches.

4 To make tiny round flowers, fold scrap paper over the desired color of felt and use a hole punch to make each circle. The paper helps the holes to punch easily. Sew into place using French knots. Make lazy-daisy stitches for leaves.

5 Fold up the pink felt to form a 3¼-inch pocket. Pin in place. Work blanket stitches around the edges, securing both layers of the pocket together.

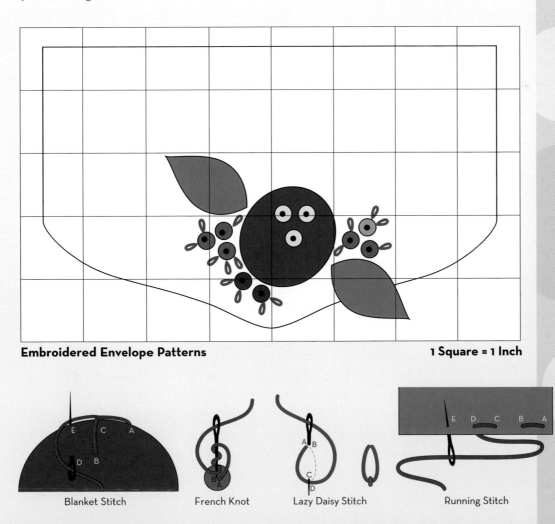

Embroidered Envelope Patterns   **1 Square = 1 Inch**

Blanket Stitch   French Knot   Lazy Daisy Stitch   Running Stitch

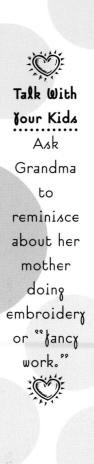

Talk With Your Kids

Ask Grandma to reminisce about her mother doing embroidery or "fancy work."

89

CREATE A CLOCK TO MATCH ANY DECOR BY USING A PICTURE FRAME AS THE CLOCK BASE. ADORN THE FACE WITH CLOTH, RIBBON, AND BUTTONS FOR A CUSTOMIZED GIFT.

Timely Frame

SUPPLIES

4-inch square of cardboard; ice pick; pencil
Battery-operated clock movement for ⅛-inch-thick clock face; fabric glue
4-inch square of fabric; scissors; 8 inches of decorative ribbon
Metal frame with 4-inch-square opening
Hot-glue gun and glue sticks; 4 decorative buttons

WHAT TO DO

1 Begin a hole in the center of the cardboard square with an ice pick. Push a pencil through the hole to enlarge it. The shaft of the clock movement should fit easily into this hole.

2 Using fabric glue, adhere the fabric square to the cardboard. Cut a tiny hole in the center of the fabric with scissors.

3 Use fabric glue to adhere pieces of ribbon horizontally and vertically, crossing in the center of the fabric. Cut a center hole in ribbons.

4 Remove backing and glass from metal frame and replace them with the fabric-covered cardboard square.

5 Follow package directions to install the clock movement through the hole in the center of the cardboard.

6 Hot-glue buttons to the four corners of the frame.

Bright Idea
......
Glue short ribbon strips to a picture frame to give it a face lift.

Sparkling Shades Case

FOR FRIENDS WHO THRIVE ON SUNSHINE, A SUNGLASS CASE IS THE JUST-RIGHT BIRTHDAY GIFT. CHOOSE A CASE IN A FAVORITE HUE AND, IN A JIFFY, MAKE IT SPECTACULAR.

SUPPLIES

Eyeglass case with
 solid-color vinyl surface
Copper wide-tip permanent marking pen
Fine-tip marking pens in silver and black
Rhinestones; gem glue

WHAT TO DO

1 Using a copper marking pen, write "shades" across the top of the eyeglass case.

2 Accent the left side of each letter by making a thin black shadow with a marking pen. Highlight the right side of each letter with silver. Using the black marker, add small dots within the copper center of each letter.

3 Glue rhinestones randomly around the lettering. Let the glue dry.

Talk With Your Kids Discuss ways to protect skin from the sun.

Zip-It-Up Pouch

SUPPLIES

Three 7-inch-long bright zippers; matching threads; sewing machine 2 black felt rectangles; ruler; scissors; blunt pencil; 1 yard purple cording

WHAT TO DO

1. Using a zipper foot on the sewing machine, sew the zippers together using narrow seams and alternating the direction of the zipper pulls.

2. Cut two 9×1¼-inch felt strips and two 5×1¼-inch long strips. Sew a 9-inch strip on each long side of zipper panel using a narrow seam. Stitch the short strips across the top and bottom of the zippers and felt strips to complete the pouch front.

3. Cut a 9×4½-inch piece of felt for the pouch back. Center and place this backing over the top of the pouch front. (Open the center zipper before placing the back over the front.) Stitch the back and front together with a narrow seam, stitching around all four sides. Clip off the corners above the stitching line and trim away any excess felt. Pull pouch right side out through the opened zipper. Use a blunt pencil to poke out the corners of the pouch.

4. Tie a knot on each end of the cording. Place a knot along the bottom of each side of the pouch and whipstitch cord to sides of pouch. The loop at the top of the pouch can be used as a shoulder strap.

BRIGHT AS A RAINBOW, THIS CONVENIENT CASE KEEPS PENS AND PENCILS ORGANIZED WITH FLAIR.

Bright Idea
......
Fashion the top of a throw pillow with zippers to make it easy to remove the pillow form.

TELL YOUR FRIENDS HOW DEAR THEY ARE WITH THIS SWEET LITTLE REMINDER. USE PAINT MARKERS FOR A QUICK DESIGN AND ACCENT THE VOTIVE CUP WITH RHINESTONES.

Message Options
Your friendship brightens each day.
••••
You mean the world to me.
••••
Believe in yourself. I do.
••••
Thank you for sharing yourself with me.
••••
I love you, dear friend!

SUPPLIES

Paper; scissors; clear glass flowerpots in 2 sizes; pencil; tape
Opaque paint markers for glass; graph paper with ¼-inch squares
Rhinestones; white glue; jelly beans; candle

Friendship Candle

WHAT TO DO

1 Cut a piece of paper to fit inside large flowerpot. You can choose a message from the list, *right*, or you can compose your own. The candle *above* says, "Roses are red. Violets are blue. No one is as sweet as a friend like you!" Arrange and write message on paper and tape it to the inside of flowerpot with message facing outward. Using paper as a guide, write message on outside of pot with paint markers.

2 Cut a strip of graph paper to fit inside the rim; tape in place. To create a checked pattern, fill in four squares with the same color to form a larger square. Skip the next four squares. Continue filling in squares in this alternating pattern.

3 Glue a rhinestone at the intersection of each large square around the center of the rim. Let the glue dry.

4 Fill flowerpot with jelly beans. Place a candle in smaller flowerpot and nestle in jelly beans.

Note: Never leave a burning candle unattended.

Designer Photo Box

As pretty as a wrapped gift and as functional as a photo album, this covered box unfolds to reveal a collection of precious snapshots.

SUPPLIES

Utility knife; 4-inch-cube box with lid
Paper to cover box; ruler; thick white crafts glue
Large needle; piece of yarn; large button
Black adhesive photo corners
Tube-style glitter paint
Large sheet of art paper in a color to complement box color

WHAT TO DO

1 Use a utility knife to cut down through all four corners of the box so it lies flat.

2 To cover each of the four sides, cut four pieces of paper each 1 inch larger in width and length than side of box. Center and glue paper to front of each side, folding excess paper to inside. Cut a piece of paper to fit the bottom of box and glue in place.

3 Calculate width and height of lid sides plus an additional ½ inch all around. Cut paper to this size. Center and glue paper to lid, folding paper over sides and around to inside edge. Cut a slit at each corner to ease the folding of the paper.

4 With a large needle punch two holes in center of lid top ⅝ inch apart. Thread yarn through holes, slip button onto yarn, tie, and clip yarn.

5 Use adhesive photo corners and glitter paint to decorate sides of lid and corners of lid top. Let dry.

6 Cut four 3⅞×15½-inch strips from art paper. Accordion-fold strips into 3⅞-inch squares. Trim excess paper at ends.

7 Glue one end of each strip to an inside panel of box. Let glue dry. Affix photo corners and photos on both sides of paper strips. If desired, secure a photo in the bottom of the box using photo corners.

Talk With Your Kids

Look through old photos and tell your children about each one. Have them take notes to record the history forever.

95

**Bright
Idea**
......
Buy an
additional
decorative
button to
make a
matching
gift card.

Baby Bundles

SUPPLIES

*Hand towel, approximately 17×29½ inches; matching thread and needle
  or sewing machine; 1 yard of ½- to 1-inch-wide embroidered trim*
Pins; baby buttons in bunny, duck, and/or flower shapes
Mini rickrack; chenille rickrack
*1 yard of 1-inch-wide ribbon or 2-inch-long strip of touch fastener, such
  as Velcro*

When a new bundle of joy arrives, celebrate the birth with a precious towel roll that keeps small objects conveniently organized.

Talk With Your Kids

Talk to your kids about how they reacted to baths as babies.

WHAT TO DO

1 Working on the right side of the towel, use a sewing machine or needle and thread to stitch the trim down the length of one long edge.

2 Lay the towel right side down, placing the embroidered trim edge at bottom. Fold the length of the bottom edge up to reveal the trim and create a 7-inch pocket. Pin and then stitch the folded towel together every 3 to 6 inches to create divided pockets. *Note:* Before stitching the edges of the first pocket on the right-hand side of the towel, arrange baby buttons and rickrack along the edge on the other (right) side of towel as shown, *opposite*. This edge will become the top of the rolled-up case. Stitch the desired arrangement of buttons and/or rickrack in place.

3 If you prefer to use ribbon to tie the case, fold the ribbon in half and insert the folded edge halfway down one side of the towel. Trap the folded ribbon in the stitches when the side edges are joined together to make the last pocket. If you choose a touch fastener to seal the case together, first stitch a scrap of trim to the back of the hook portion of the touch fastener. Insert one edge of this tab halfway down the edge of the towel. Trap the end of the tab in stitches when the side edges are joined together to make the last pocket. To gauge the placement of the loop portion of the touch fastener, insert various items into the finished pockets. When the case is rolled up, position the loop portion to fall under the hook tab and then stitch it in place.

Bright Idea
Give dimension to the place mats by using buttons for the flower centers.

WHETHER YOU MAKE ONE FOR A DRESSER OR A SET FOR THE KITCHEN, THIS COLORFUL MAT DELIVERS A RAINBOW OF JOY-FILLED WISHES.

Blooming Place Mat

SUPPLIES

Decorative-edge scissors; crafts foam in light green, medium green, yellow, turquoise, pink, light orange, orange, and purple; ruler; scissors Thick white crafts glue; tracing paper; pencil; scrap paper; hole punch

WHAT TO DO

1 Using decorative-edge scissors, trim the light green crafts foam to 11½×15 inches. Glue the green piece on top of a larger piece of yellow foam. Let dry.

2 Trim the sides of the yellow foam with decorative-edge scissors and the top and bottom, if necessary, with straight-edge scissors.

3 Enlarge and trace desired patterns, *pages 100–101*. Cut out patterns. Trace around patterns on desired colors of crafts foam. Using the placement diagram, *below*, as a guide, glue several flowers to one corner. Arrange flower centers and leaves as desired. Glue one or two flowers in the opposite corner.

4 To make small dots, fold a piece of scrap paper in half and sandwich the edge of a piece of crafts foam between the paper layers. Using a hole punch, punch out dots. Glue foam dots in place. Let the glue dry.

continued on page 100

Blooming Place Mat Placement Diagram

99

Blooming Place Mat
Patterns

**Blooming Place Mat
Patterns**

Talk With
Your Kids
Discuss
all the
happenings
of the
day at
dinnertime.

101

Bright Idea

Glue groups of clay flowers to larger containers and use them as kitchen canisters.

ADORNED WITH ZANY CLAY FLOWERS, POLKA DOTS, AND COLORFUL BANDING, THESE LITTLE TINS ARE THE IDEAL SIZE FOR ORGANIZING A KITCHEN OR OFFICE.

Trinket Tins

SUPPLIES

Small tins (available in crafts stores or as spice tins in discount stores)
Oven-bake clay, such as Sculpey; baking sheet; paper clip
Large seed beads; rolling pin; ruler; crafts knife
Scallop-edge scissors; strong clear adhesive, such as Liquid Nails

WHAT TO DO

1. For each tin, form a small clay flower to fit the lid. Roll small balls or ovals as petals, or roll a long rope and coil it. Join a desired center to each flower. Place flowers on a baking sheet.

2. To make leaves, roll a small ball. Flatten it slightly and shape into a leaf. Flatten again if necessary. Press to clay flower.

3. To make indentations, use a paper clip. Use the rounded end to add vein lines or the tip of a paper clip to poke small holes.

4. To make polka dots for the tin, make pea-size balls from clay. Place on baking sheet. Press a seed bead in the center of each piece of clay.

5. To create a dotted band for the tin, roll out a piece of clay until it is approximately ⅛ inch thick. Use a ruler and a crafts knife to cut one straight edge. Carefully lift the clay up and cut a scalloped edge ½ inch from the straight edge. Wrap around tin, positioning it to avoid interfering with the placement of the lid. Press a seed bead into every other scallop.

6. To make a twisted rope trim for the tin base, choose two colors of clay. Roll each into thin ropes. Twist the ropes together. Place twisted rope around the tin base as desired. Cut away excess clay. Press seed beads into clay where desired.

7. Bake the clay-covered tin and clay pieces following the manufacturer's instructions. Let cool. Glue clay pieces on the tins. Let the glue dry.

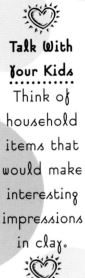

Talk With Your Kids
Think of household items that would make interesting impressions in clay.

103

RECYCLE PLASTIC AND GLASS BOTTLES BY TURNING THEM INTO SNAZZY VASES! WIND EMBROIDERY FLOSS CAREFULLY AROUND A BOTTLE TO MAKE STRIPES OR WRAP IT UNEVENLY TO CREATE A VASE THAT IS LOADED WITH COLOR AND TEXTURE.

Color-Wrapped Vases

SUPPLIES

Glass or plastic bottle; thick white crafts glue; embroidery floss

WHAT TO DO

1. Wash the bottle. Let it dry. Place a dot of glue at the bottom edge of the bottle. Begin wrapping the embroidery floss around the bottle, keeping the wraps close together and applying more dots of glue when needed. To change colors, cut the floss and glue the end in place.

2. Continue making stripes of color like this until the entire bottle is covered with floss. Let the glue dry.

Go Fishing Frame

SUPPLIES

5×7-inch wood photo frame; sandpaper
Acrylic paints in blue, white, and assorted fish colors
Paintbrush; paint sponge; wave stencil
Tracing paper; pencil; scissors; white mat board
Sequins in assorted sizes and colors
Thick white crafts glue; crafts knife
3/16-inch-diameter dowel; metallic cording
Adhesive dots (2 for each fish)

WHAT TO DO

1. Sand the frame and paint it blue. Allow the paint to dry. Use the paint sponge and white paint to stencil the frame with waves.

2. Trace the fish patterns, *below*, onto tracing paper; cut out. Cut out the shapes from mat board. Paint the fish in assorted paint colors. Glue sequins in place.

3. Use a crafts knife to cut four dowel lengths for fishing poles. Tie a length of metallic cording to the end of each pole for fishing line. Place adhesive dots (two dots stacked together) on the back of each fish. Press the fish to the frame. Glue poles to the frame and cording ends to the fish.

THIS FRAME NETS A BIG CATCH OF KUDOS WITH SEQUINS, STENCILING, AND WOOD DOWELS.

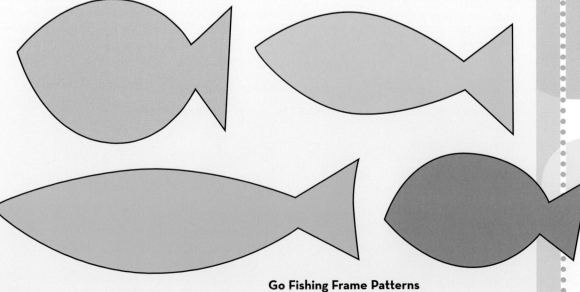

Go Fishing Frame Patterns

Talk With Your Kids

Discuss the various types of fish found in salt water.

Precious Blooms

SUPPLIES

Acrylic paints; paintbrush; 4-inch-diameter terra-cotta pots; sharp knife
Thick white crafts glue; pressed flowers; florist's foam; scissors; ruler
Green tissue and crepe papers; pencil; tracing paper; card stock in
  assorted colors and white; photos; dotted green scrapbook paper
Alphabet stamps; black ink pad; 18-gauge green plastic-coated wire
Scallop-edge scissors; magenta marking pen; seeds

WHAT TO DO

1 Paint the pots. Glue pressed flowers to the rims. Use a knife to cut disks of florist's foam and place inside each pot.

2 For grass, cut 5-inch strips from tissue and crepe papers. Snip across the strips at ¼-inch intervals, making cuts about 2 inches deep. Stack the strips and roll up. Place the "grass" inside each pot.

3 Trace the patterns, *opposite;* cut out. Cut flowers from card stock. Cut circles from photos. Cut seed packets from dotted green paper.

4 Glue photos to the flowers. Stamp herb names on the petals. Cut wire double the desired length for stems. Place wire center over a pencil and twist ends together until the full length is twisted. Remove pencil; glue wire stem to flower.

5 Fold seed packets along fold lines. Glue flaps at the center back and bottom. Cut labels from white card stock; stamp with herb names. Trim labels with scallop-edge scissors. Color the label edges magenta; glue to front of seed packet. Fill packet with seeds; glue each top flap closed.

PUT YOUR FRESH FACE ON A PLANT MARKER SO IT CAN "FLOWER" AMONG THE HERBS.

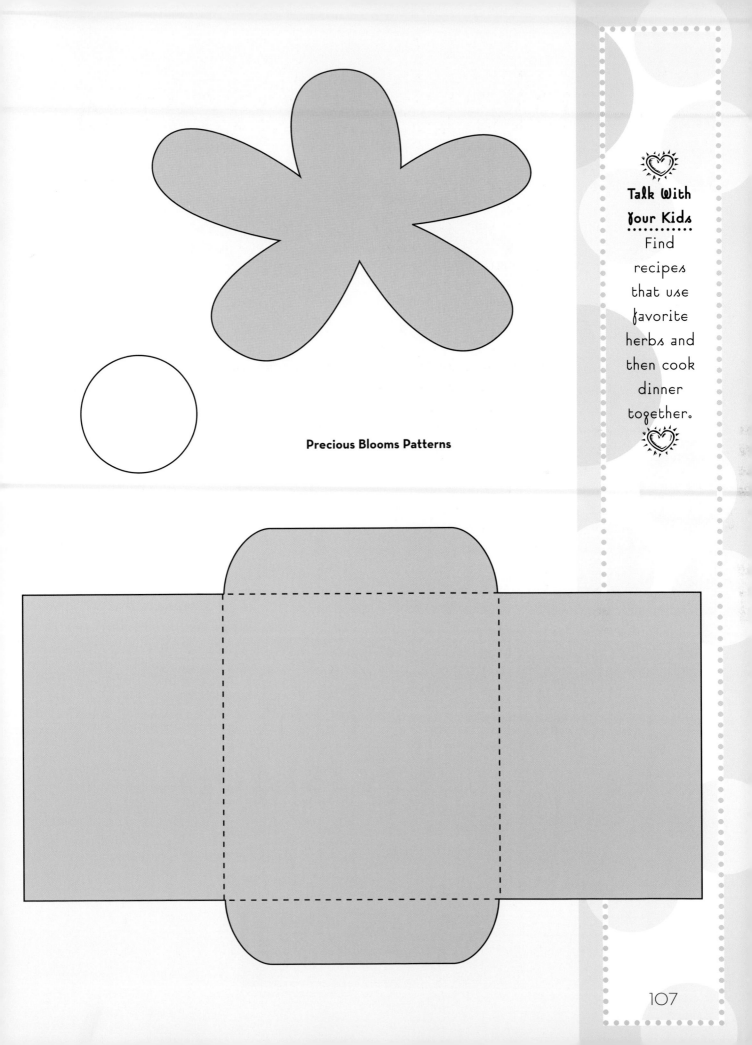

Precious Blooms Patterns

Fun to Wear

With rings for your toes and hats for your head,
this chapter is brimming with ideas to make together for
stylish fashion fun.

**Bright
Idea**
Tie-dye
white
sheets
and a
pillowcase
to brighten
up your
bed.

Tie-dye T-shirts

The fun of tie-dyeing is that every project is different and an anticipated surprise! So find some old clothes and get ready to splash a white t-shirt with all your favorite colors!

SUPPLIES

White shirt; tie-dye kit
Bucket; rubber bands

WHAT TO DO

1 To tie-dye the shirt, follow the directions on the tie-dye kit.

2 To make a stripe design, fold the shirt back and forth as shown in Photo A, *right*. To make an allover design, twist the shirt as shown in Photos B and C. Wrap shirts with rubber bands.

3 Dye the wrapped shirt as shown in Photo D, following the manufacturer's directions.

4 Let the shirt set according to the dye instructions. Remove the rubber bands as shown in Photo E. Rinse, wash, and dry the shirt.

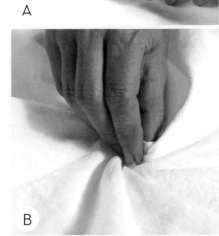

A

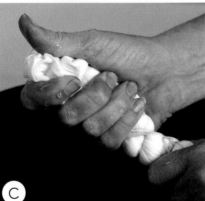

B

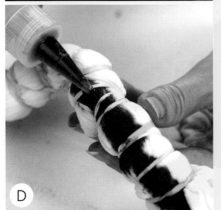

C

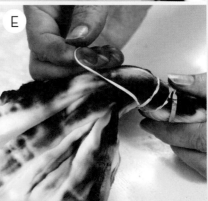

D

E

Talk With Your Kids

Get to know the color wheel by talking about colors and how they mix.

Bright Idea

Personalize a canvas book bag using permanent marking pens.

FRIENDS' NAMES LOOK REALLY NEAT—ESPECIALLY WHEN THEY'RE ON YOUR FEET! INVITE YOUR FRIENDS TO WRITE THEIR NAMES ON YOUR SHOES WITH COLORFUL MARKING PENS.

SUPPLIES

Purchased canvas tennis shoes
Permanent marking pens
Crafts glue; colorful jewels
Yarn in bright colors; scissors

WHAT TO DO

1 Have friends write their names on the tennis shoes using permanent marking pens.

2 Using crafts glue, stick jewels around the names and on other parts of the shoes. Let the glue dry.

3 Cut the yarn the length of shoelaces. Thread the yarn through the lace holes and tie as shoelaces.

Autograph Shoes

Super-Duper Sunglasses

SUPPLIES

Sunglasses; acrylic enamel paints; small paintbrush

WHAT TO DO

1. When planning how to paint your glasses, look at the different parts of the frames. Paint each part a different color if you like.

2. If possible, take the lenses out of the frames to avoid getting paint on them. Paint the main color and let it dry. Paint it two or three times. Make sure the paint is dry before applying another coat of paint.

3. Paint stripes or dots in different colors. Use a tiny paintbrush to make stripes. Use the handle of the paintbrush to make dots. Let the paint dry.

Talk With Your Kids

Talk about visits to the eye doctor and how to keep eyes healthy.

MAKE ORDINARY SUNGLASSES REALLY SUN-SATIONAL BY DASHING AND DOTTING BRIGHT PAINT ON THE RIMS.

Beaded Blooms

Bright Idea
......
Poke a stickpin through the brim of a hat.

SUPPLIES FOR THE PINK FLOWER PIN

Colorful button with a shank
30 inches of fine wire that will hold its shape with seed beads on it
Scissors; pink seed beads; 5 purple accent beads
Adhesive, such as Krazy Glue Gel; lapel pin with pad

WHAT TO DO

1 Tie one end of wire into the button shank, leaving the bottom side of the shank clear of wire for easy gluing to the pin later.

2 Thread about 2 inches of seed beads onto the wire, an accent bead, and another 2 inches of seed beads. Pull the wire back through the shank to make a petal. Shape the petal any way you want.

3 Continue threading beads to make four more petals, pulling the wire back through the shank until all petals are complete. Trim wire ends.

4 Use a generous amount of adhesive on the flat side of the shank and place it on the pad of the lapel pin.

SUPPLIES FOR THE BLUE AND GREEN FLOWER PIN

Button with 2 or 4 holes; three 6-inch pieces of fine wire
Gold spacer bead; bead for flower center
  (6 wires must fit through hole); assorted small beads
Adhesive, such as Krazy Glue Gel; lapel pin with pad

WHAT TO DO

1 Insert each wire through a buttonhole to the back side and back through the front side. Six wires will extend through the top side of the button, each about 3 inches long.

2 Place a spacer bead over the wires first and then thread the bead for flower center; pull all wires through both beads.

3 String each wire with assorted beads until almost full. Thread on each final bead and twist the remainder of each wire several times until the bead is held firmly in place; trim extra wire.

4 Use a generous amount of adhesive on the back side of the button and place it on the pad of the lapel pin. Let dry until it is very secure.

BEADS PARADE AS PETALED FLOWERS ON EASY-TO-SHAPE CRAFTS WIRE.

ROLL AND WRAP CLAY TO MAKE THE
PRETTIEST BRACELET AROUND.

Clay Crazy

SUPPLIES

Oven-bake clay, such as Sculpey; waxed paper
Small straw; baking dish; scissors
Heavy elastic string; ruler

WHAT TO DO

1 To make a round bead, pinch off a marble-size piece from clay. Roll it into a ball.

2 To twist colors, pinch off a pea-size piece from a different color of clay. Roll the clay into a thin snake shape. Wrap the snake piece around the ball, pressing it into place.

3 To make polka dots, pinch off tiny pieces of clay. Roll each piece into a ball. Press onto the larger clay ball.

4 To make a flat bead, pinch off a pea-size piece of clay. Flatten with palm of hand on a piece of waxed paper.

5 To make a hole in each bead, press a straw through the center and remove. Place the clay beads on a baking dish. Bake the clay pieces in the oven following the package directions. Let cool.

6 Cut a piece of elastic 5 inches larger than your wrist. String beads on elastic until about 4 inches of the elastic is left. Knot the elastic ends together. Trim the ends of the elastic.

Talk With Your Kids
Talk about what might make good organizers for jewelry.

Birdy Cap

SUPPLIES

Tracing paper; pencil; scissors; crafts foam in yellow, white, and black
Thick white crafts glue; heavy book; baseball cap; bobby pins
Large colored feather; tape; ball to fit in cap

WHAT TO DO

1 Trace the patterns, *opposite* and *page 118*, onto tracing paper. Cut out the patterns and trace onto foam. Cut out the foam shapes.

2 Using a small amount of glue, stick the black pupils and eyebrows onto the white eyeballs. Change the position of the black foam pieces to make different expressions. Put the pupils close together and the eyes one above the other to make the bird look cross-eyed. Place the pupils in the center for a look of surprise. Move the pupils to the bottom to make the bird look down or on the top to make the bird look up. Set a heavy book on the pieces until dry.

3 Glue the beak onto the bill of the cap. Use bobby pins to hold it in place while the glue dries.

4 Tape the large feather to the middle of the front of the cap.

5 Place the hat over a ball to give it shape while finishing the face. Glue on the eyes and tape them in place while drying. When all the glue is dry, remove the tape from the eyes and ball.

*continued on
page 118*

**Birdy Cap
Eye Patterns**

Birdy Cap Diagram

**Talk With
Your Kids**
Look
online to
find out
how many
species of
birds exist
and how
many are
endangered.

Go ahead—flap your
arms and squawk
like a bird! When
you wear this
crazy cap, act
as loony as
you like!

Birdy Cap continued

Birdy Cap Beak Pattern

DESIGN A SWEET CARRYALL THAT'S PERFECT FOR TOTING YOUR TUTU AND DANCE SHOES! WITH A FEW STEPS, COMPLETE YOUR VERY OWN BALLET BAG.

Beautiful Ballet Bag

SUPPLIES

Mesh tote bag; 24 hair clips
6 ball-style ponytail holders; scissors

WHAT TO DO

1 Fasten five hair clips between the handles on each side of the bag.

2 Cut two ponytail holders in half. Thread the ends of one half through two holes in the center of the mesh bag. Knot the ends on the inside of the bag.

3 Tie on the three other ponytail holder halves close to the first one. Wrap a whole ponytail holder around those tied to the bag. Snap seven hair clips around the ponytail holders.

4 Turn over the bag and repeat Steps 2–3.

Talk With Your Kids
Discuss what kinds of dance moves they like. Have them turn on their favorite music and show you!

Bright Idea
......
Thread fringe with pony beads, knotting fringe ends to hold them in place.

Adorable Denim

SUPPLIES FOR THE PURSE

Two 3-inch squares of denim; scissors
Iron-on sun-motif embroidery, such as Dritz Soleil; iron
Fray stop, such as Dritz Fray-N-Stay; denim purse, approximately
  8×9 inches; antique brass star eyelets
Eyelet tool; 2 packages of natural leather lacing

WHAT TO DO

1 Wash the denim squares without fabric softener. Dry the denim. Cut two sun designs from the iron-on embroidery sheet. Iron one to each denim square.

2 Fray the denim squares and secure with fray stop. Referring to the photo, *above*, attach each square to the purse with a star eyelet.

3 Cut two 9-inch lengths of lacing. Fold one length in half; push the fold through the star eyelet on one denim square. Cut the lacing fold and tie the two lengths in a knot behind the eyelet. Repeat for other lacing length and denim square.

4 Attach eight star eyelets across the top of the purse front. Cut one 16-inch length of lacing for each eyelet. Thread and knot the lacing as directed in Step 3.

SUPPLIES FOR THE KEY CLIP

Scissors; ruler; denim; cobalt blue suede leather lacing
Fray stop, such as Dritz Fray-N-Stay; lanyard hook; 16-mm split ring
Fabric glue; four ³⁄₈-inch-long polymer clay tube beads with large holes
  or any beads with large holes
4 silver spacer beads with large holes

WHAT TO DO

1 Cut three ½×10-inch strips of denim and two 10-inch lengths of the suede leather lacing. For ease, make a tiny snip in the denim; rip the rest of the strip length. Fray the denim strips and secure with fray stop.

2 Slide the lanyard hook onto the split ring. Place the denim strips in a neat stack. Use light dabs of fabric glue to hold the denim strips together at one end. Fold 1 inch of the glued denim end over the split ring. Wrap a lacing length around the six strips of denim just outside the split ring. Tie the lacing in a tight knot.

3 Braid the denim strips. Tie the remaining lacing length around the bottom of the braid and knot. Thread one bead and one spacer on each lacing end; knot the end of each lacing length and trim as desired.

SUPPLIES FOR THE PRETTY CHOKER

Scissors; ruler; fray stop, such as Dritz Fray-N-Stay
Bright suede leather lacing
Water-soluble fabric marking pen or a pencil
Silver spacer beads with large holes
Six ³⁄₈-inch-long polymer clay tube beads with large holes
  or any beads with large holes

WHAT TO DO

1 Cut a 1×10-inch strip of denim. For ease make a tiny snip in the denim; rip the rest of the strip. Fray the strip and secure it with fray stop. Cut a 32-inch length of lacing.

2 Using the marking pen, make dots along the center of the denim as follows: Starting at one end, measure ³⁄₈ inch and mark a dot; make three more dots ³⁄₈ inch apart. Measure 1 inch and mark a dot. Repeat the measuring sequence described five more times. Then measure out and mark the rest of the denim in ³⁄₈-inch lengths.

3 Fold the denim in half lengthwise so dots are visible. Cut small slits in the fold at each dot. Thread the lacing from the back of the denim through the first slit, insert a silver spacer, and thread the lacing down

continued on page 122

121

through the next slit. Bring the lacing up through the next slit and insert a spacer, a bead, and a spacer. Thread the lacing down through the next slit. Repeat this spacer-bead-spacer sequence five more times. Finish the lacing with a spacer. Tie choker around neck.

SUPPLIES FOR THE APPLIQUÉD JEANS

Seam ripper; denim jeans; scissors; fray stop, such as Dritz Fray-N-Stay; hook-and-eye closure; needle and thread Dritz Easy Bleach; 1 or 2 packages of iron-on embroidery, such as Dritz Lotus Butterfly; iron

WHAT TO DO

1 Using a seam ripper, remove the cuff hems on jeans. Cut away the waistband. Fringe the cut edges to the desired length and secure with fray stop. Sew a hook-and-eye closure slightly above the zipper.

2 Wash the jeans without fabric softener. Follow the instructions for the Distressed Denim technique on the Easy Bleach package.

3 Cut out the embroidery elements. Position them on the jeans and press with an iron, following the package instructions.

SUPPLIES FOR THE MINISKIRT

Seam ripper; denim skirt
Fray stop, such as Dritz Fray-N-Stay; Dritz Easy Bleach Marbles; rubber bands; brown leather lacing; scissors

WHAT TO DO

1 Using a seam ripper, remove the skirt hem. Fringe the bottom edge to the desired length and secure with fray stop.

2 Wash the skirt without fabric softener. Leave the skirt damp. Follow the Tie-Dye Small Circles instructions

described on the Easy Bleach package using marbles and rubber bands.

3 Cut the leather lacing in two strips to fit around the waistband. Knot the lacing strips in the front.

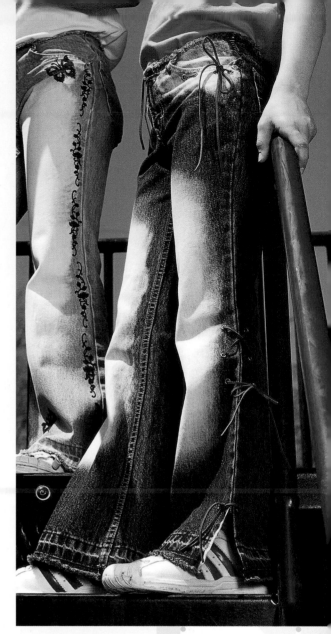

SUPPLIES FOR THE LEATHER-LACED JEANS

Seam ripper; denim jeans; scissors
Fray stop, such as Dritz Fray-N-Stay
Needle and thread; hook-and-eye closure
30 copper eyelets; eyelet tool; ruler
2 packages of brown leather lacing

WHAT TO DO

1 Using a seam ripper, remove cuff hems from jeans. Cut away the waistband. Fringe the cut edges to the desired length and secure with fray stop. Sew a hook-and-eye closure slightly above the zipper. Wash the jeans without using fabric softener. Dry the jeans.

2 Attach eyelets to the jeans, placing six eyelets along the edge of each front pocket and one on each side of the zipper. On each outside leg seam, measure up 4 inches from the cuff hem. Attach a pair of eyelets, placing one on each side of the seam, ³/₄ inch from the seam. Referring to the photo, *right*, midway on each outside leg seam, attach three pairs of eyelets as directed for the leg cuffs, spacing them 1¹/₂ inches apart.

3 For leather lacing, cut two 12-inch lengths for the leg cuff eyelet pairs, two 31-inch lengths for the mid-leg eyelets, two 15-inch and two 18-inch lengths for the pocket eyelets, and one 16-inch length for the zipper eyelets. Set the lengths of lacing aside.

4 Use scissors to make a 4-inch cut up the outside edge of each leg cuff. Fringe the cut edges and secure with fray stop. Thread one lacing length through each pair of eyelets and knot to secure. Thread the 31-inch lacing length through the mid-leg eyelets as you would a pair of sneakers. Tie the ends in a bow.

5 Knot one end on each of the four pocket lacings. To lace one pocket, thread an 18-inch lacing length through the top pocket eyelet from the inside. Weave the lacing in and out of the eyelets, stopping at the fifth eyelet. Thread a 15-inch length through the sixth eyelet with the knot inside the pocket. Tie the lacings together in a bow.

6 Repeat Step 5 for other pocket. Thread the 16-inch length of lacing through the zipper eyelets and knot.

Talk With
Your Kids
Show them
how to do
the laundry
and let
them help
with the
task.

123

Tippy-Toe Rings

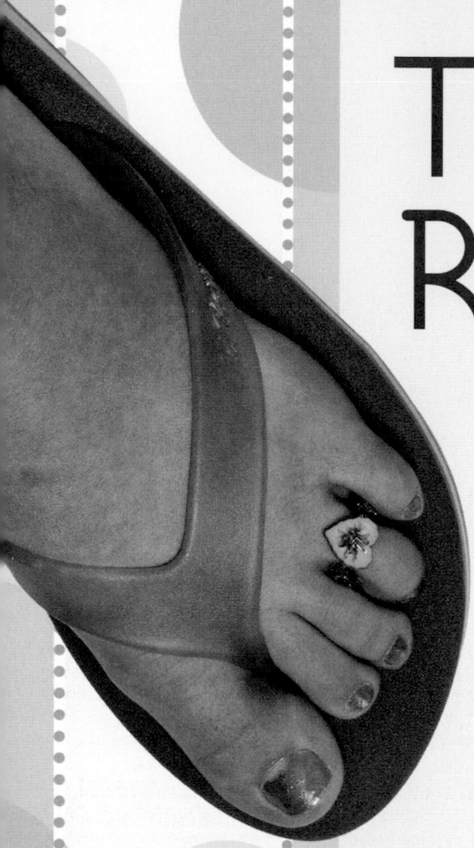

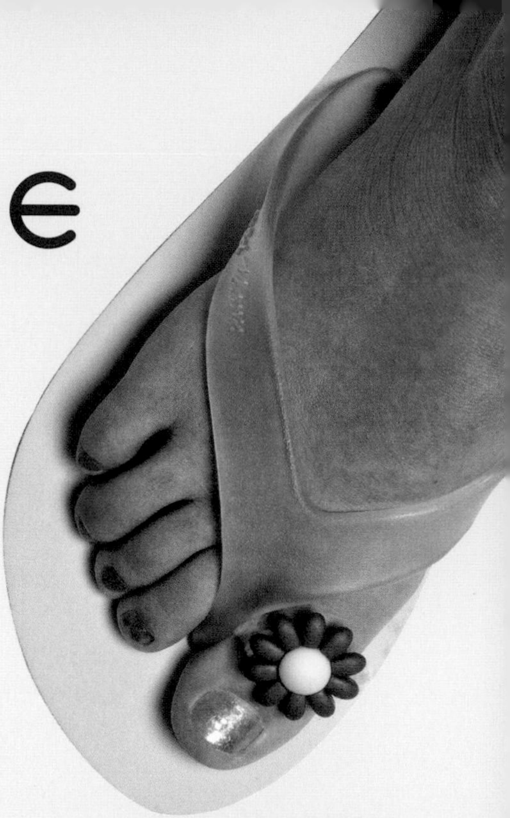

SUPPLIES

Chenille stems
Assorted decorative items,
such as beads, buttons, and
foam shapes; scissors

WHAT TO DO

1 For each ring, thread a chenille stem with one or more decorative items.

2 Wrap the chenille stem in a ring around a toe. Remove the ring. Wrap the chenille stem ends around the ring and trim any excess.

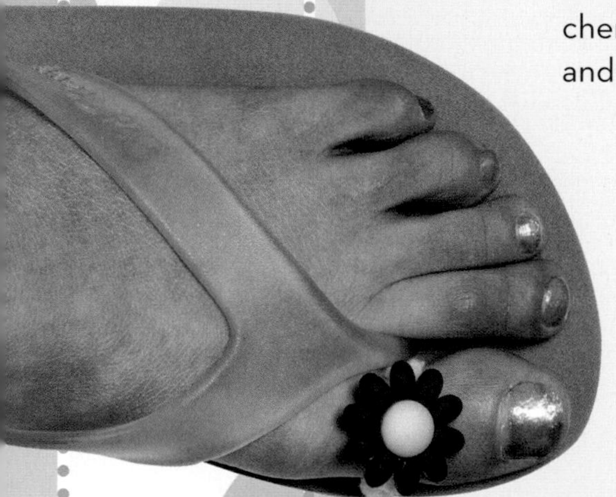

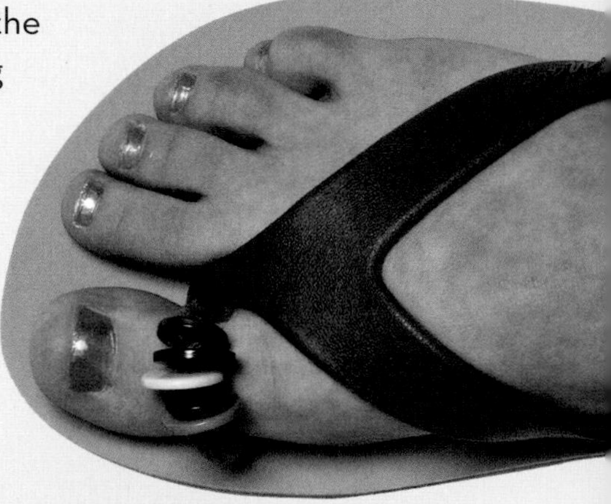

GO WILD MAKING LITTLE DOODADS TO TRIM YOUR TOES. THEY TAKE ONLY SECONDS TO MAKE!

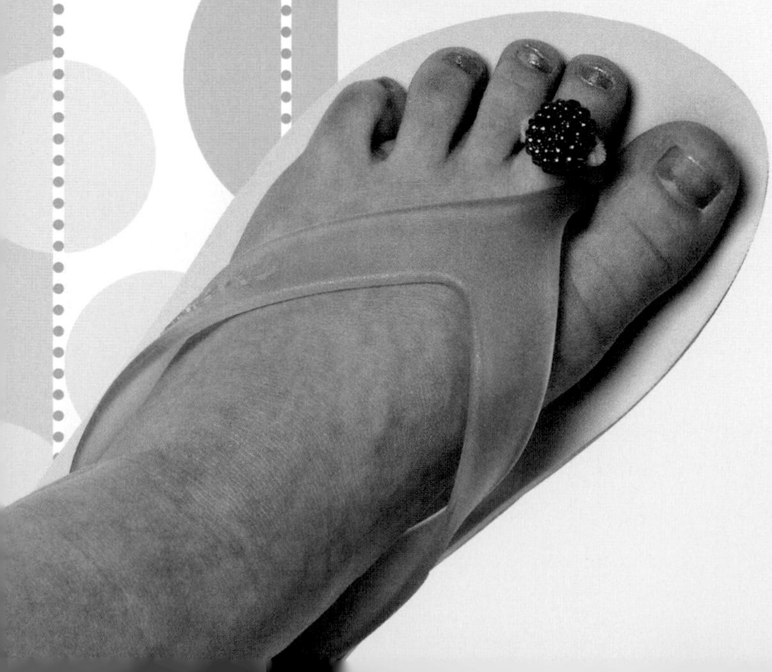

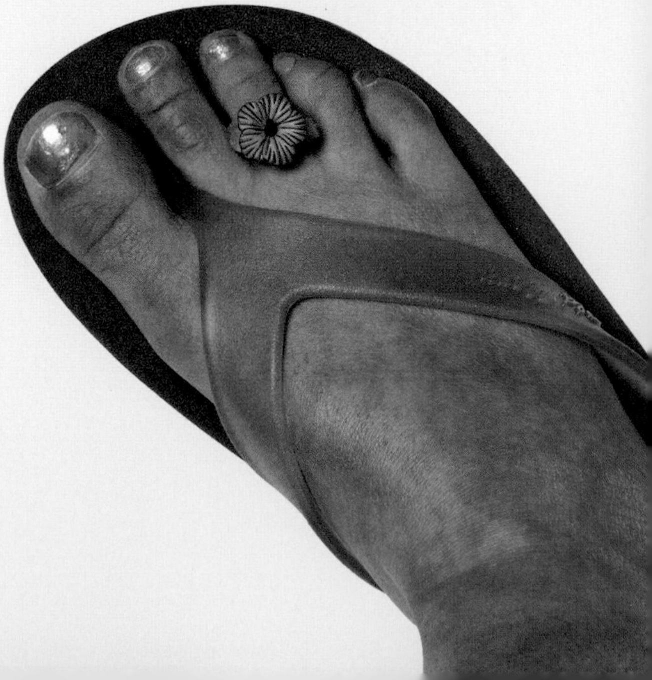

VISIT THE SCRAPBOOK STORE AND PICK UP TAGS, BRADS, STICKERS, AND CHARMS TO PERSONALIZE YOUR BELT.

SUPPLIES

Black woven leather belt
Black embroidery floss; needle
6-inch piece of chain (can be a bracelet with clasp removed)
Metal-edge tags and metal initials (available in scrapbook stores)
Alphabet sticker
Small photo
Scissors
Decorative brads (available in scrapbook stores)
Large silver-tone beads

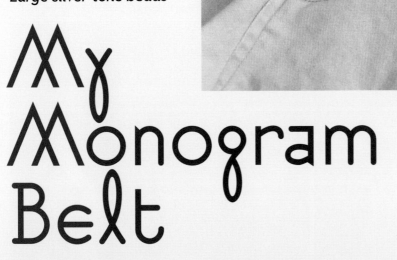

My Monogram Belt

WHAT TO DO

1 Thread belt through pant loops to determine positioning of trims. Sew one end of chain close to the belt buckle.

2 Arrange metal-edge tags on belt and chain and decide where to place metal initials, alphabet sticker, and photo. Trim the photo to fit the desired tag.

3 To secure the tags in place, use a brad or embroidery floss and a bead. Stitch on additional tags with beads where desired. Secure brads randomly around belt.

Talk With Your Kids
Tell them why and how you chose their names.

125

Winter Warmers

Bright Idea

Make a mitten and hat set by edging both with buttons, charms, pom-poms, or other trims.

SLIP INTO THESE TOASTY ACCESSORIES AND STAY COMFY WHETHER YOU'RE INSIDE GABBING WITH YOUR FRIENDS OR OUTSIDE BUILDING A SNOW FORT WITH THE FAMILY NEXT DOOR.

SUPPLIES

Socks; pom-poms; fabric trims; fabric glue
Mittens; thread; needle; scissors
Charms or buttons

WHAT TO DO

1 To trim the socks, glue pom-poms or fabric trims around the cuff in a pattern or randomly. Let the glue dry.

2 To trim the mittens, sew charms or buttons to the cuffs. Knot the thread on the wrong side.

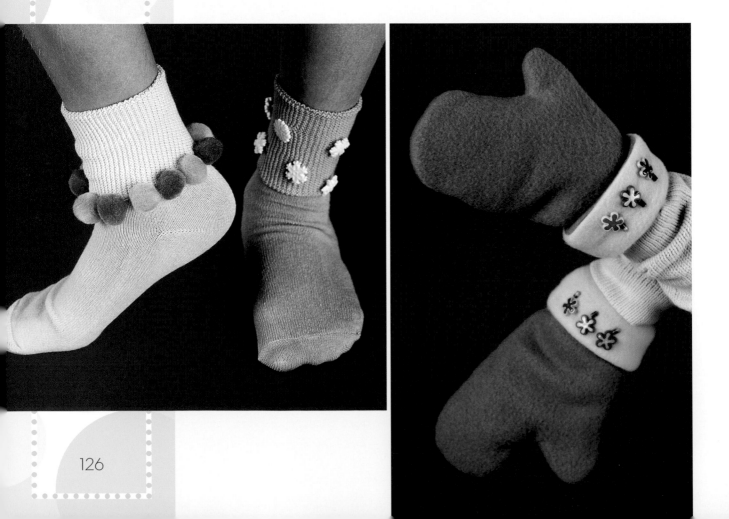

Holiday Socks

SUPPLIES
Water-soluble fabric pen or tailor's chalk
Assorted trims: snowflake buttons, pom-poms, or 3-ply crewel yarn
Scissors
Large-eye plastic needle
Socks

WHAT TO DO

1 Draw a holiday design on the foot of each sock using the water-soluble fabric pen for light-colored socks or tailor's chalk for dark-color socks.

2 Separate the three-ply crewel yarn and thread the plastic needle with two plies. Stitch the designs with running stitches and straight stitches. To end the design, weave the yarn in and out of stitches inside the sock for at least 1 inch. Knot and trim the yarn.

KEEP YOUR TOES COZY WITH JOLLY SOCKS STITCHED WITH SYMBOLS OF THE SEASON. THESE STRIKING SOCKS ALSO MAKE A GREAT GIFT.

Talk With Your Kids

Discuss types of projects to make for everyone on your family's holiday gift list.

127

Pom-Pom Pretties

Bright Idea
......
Make a matching purse to complete the ensemble.

SUPPLIES

Plastic bag
Felt beret-style hat
Assorted sizes of pom-poms
Fabric glue
Felt scarf

WHAT TO DO

1 Tuck a plastic bag into the beret to prevent the glue from soaking through. Lay the beret and scarf on a flat surface.

2 Arrange pom-poms on beret. Put a large pom-pom in the center and smaller ones around the edge. Arrange the pom-poms in rows, group colors, or make any pattern you wish.

3 One at a time, remove the pom-poms, apply a large amount of fabric glue, and press back onto the hat. Decorate the scarf in the same way. When one side of the scarf is done and dry, turn it over and do the other side. Let the glue dry.

LIKE A COLOR WHEEL, THIS HAT AND SCARF SET IS SPLASHED WITH ALL THE COLORS OF A RAINBOW.

SUPPLIES

Scissors; cardboard; gloves; needle and thread to match gloves
Sequins, beads, and buttons; fabric glue; fake-fur trim

WHAT TO DO

1 Cut a piece of cardboard to fit into the palm of the glove or mitten. Slip it inside. To sew on sequins, beads, and buttons, prepare needle with thread to match gloves. Use a double strand about 12 inches long. Knot the end.

2 Insert the needle where you want to attach a bead, button, or sequin. Catch the surface of the glove and sew a small stitch. Stitch two or three times as shown in Photo A, *below.* String the item onto the needle and insert the needle back into the glove as shown in Photo B. After the item is sewed on, make two or three more stitches in the glove fabric; trim off extra thread.

3 Cut fur to fit around each wrist area. Glue in place; let dry.

Fashion Gloves

GET A GLAMOROUS LOOK WITH A
FEW QUICK STITCHES AND TRIMS.

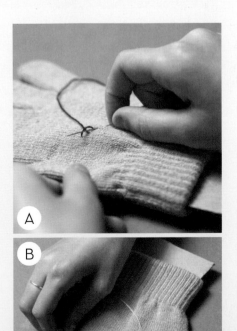

A

B

Talk With Your Kids
Discuss what types of things you like to do in cold weather.

Bright Idea
......
Tie tiny toys onto your flip-flops, such as plastic rings, game pieces, and dolls.

Beach Flip-Flops

SUPPLIES

Solid-color flip-flops; bright pink acrylic enamel paint
Paintbrush; white sparkle yarn; ruler; scissors; crafts glue
³/₄-inch-wide sheer white ribbon; bright pink metallic curling ribbon

WHAT TO DO

1 Paint vertical stripes on the edge of each flip-flop. Let the paint dry.

2 Cut two 24-inch-long pieces of yarn. Glue one end of the yarn to the underside of the plastic strap where it meets the bottom of the flip-flop. Wrap the entire strap with yarn. Trim away the extra yarn. Glue yarn end to back side of plastic strap. Let dry. Repeat for the other flip-flop.

3 Tie a small ribbon bow for each flip-flop. Use curling ribbon to tie a bow to the top of each flip-flop.

FEEL LIKE A PRINCESS AT THE BEACH OR AT THE POOL WITH THESE FANCY SANDALS ON YOUR FEET.

Glitter Hats

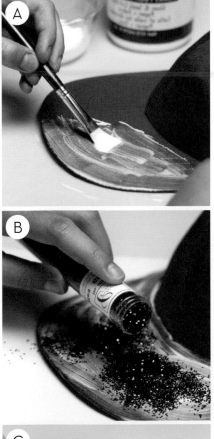

PUT SPARKLE IN EVERYONE'S EYES WITH THESE FUN-TO-MAKE CAPS THAT SINE FROM THE GLISTENING SUN'S RAYS!

Talk With Your Kids
Do some hat research together. Find out what styles have been popular throughout time.

SUPPLIES
Waxed paper; decoupage medium; paintbrush; baseball cap
Glitter or confetti; gold glitter fabric paint; jewels with flat backs

WHAT TO DO

1 Cover your work surface with waxed paper. Use a paintbrush to paint the entire bill of the cap with a thick coat of decoupage medium.

2 Sprinkle glitter or confetti onto the decoupage medium until the bill is well-covered.

3 Squeeze small dabs of gold fabric paint onto the rest of the cap. Press the jewels into the paint while it is still wet. Make small lines of paint around the jewels if you wish. Let the cap dry.

4 Paint over the glitter with decoupage medium to seal it. Let the cap dry before wearing.

Bright Idea
· · · · · ·
Use painted spools as legs for papier-mâché boxes.

SUPPLIES

Newspapers; wood spools and/or small spools with thread on them
Black acrylic paint; paintbrush; wood beads; paint markers
Colored string; scissors; colored plastic beads in a variety of shapes

WHAT TO DO

1. Cover the work surface with newspapers. Paint the wood spools black, leaving one end unpainted. Set each spool on the unpainted end until dry.

2. Turn the spools over and paint the remaining end. Let them dry. Paint the wood beads black. Let dry.

3. Using paint markers, draw dots or other basic designs on the black spools. Let dry.

4. Cut a piece of string long enough for a necklace, including about 4 inches for tying. Thread the string with painted beads, plastic beads, painted spools and/or spools with thread in the order you want. When the string is almost full, knot the ends together. Cut off the extra string.

Nifty Necklace

MAKE A PRETTY NECKLACE TO WEAR WITH YOUR FAVORITE CLOTHES. PICK THE COLORS AND GET BUSY PAINTING!

Graphic Jewelry

SUPPLIES

Tracing paper; pencil; scissors
Crafts foam in desired colors
Decorative-edge scissors; large hole punch
Triangle punch
Foam glue, such as Hold the Foam; gems
Gem glue; cord; pinch-style jewelry clasp; charm
Safety pins; needle; string; beads

WHAT TO DO

1 Trace the desired patterns, *pages 134–135*, and cut them out. Trace around the patterns on foam. Read through all steps before gluing.

2 Using the photos, *right*, as guides, cut out the shapes using straight or decorative-edge scissors. Use punches to make dots or triangle cutouts.

3 For layered jewelry, glue the shapes together. Embellish with gems if desired.

4 For the necklaces, fold over the tab to the back and secure tip with glue; let dry. Thread cord through loop.

5 For the pinch-clasp bracelet, layer three narrow foam strips and secure one end in the clasp. Repeat for the other end. Attach the jump ring on the charm to the clasp.

6 For the flower pin, avoid gluing the leaf area around and between the punched dots. Thread a safety pin through the punched holes in the leaves.

7 For the flower bracelet, slip a large bead on the narrow end of the foam strip. To wear, wrap bracelet around wrist and push the bead through the slit in the center of the flower to secure.

8 For the triangle cutout bracelet, glue a foam strip under the cutouts; let dry. Cut two 5-inch-long pieces of string. From the inside of the bracelet, sew a large bead on the narrow end of the bracelet; knot on the back. String a small bead on each thread; knot ends to prevent beads from slipping off.

continued on page 134

Talk With Your Kids

Talk about jewelry styles throughout history.

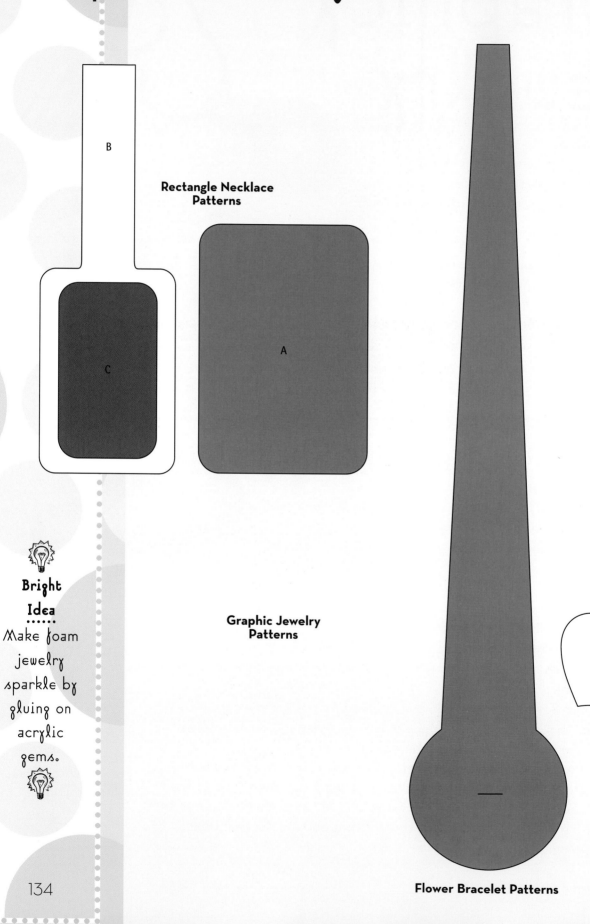

Rectangle Necklace Patterns

B

C

A

Graphic Jewelry Patterns

Bright Idea
······
Make foam jewelry sparkle by gluing on acrylic gems.

Flower Bracelet Patterns

Flower Pin Patterns

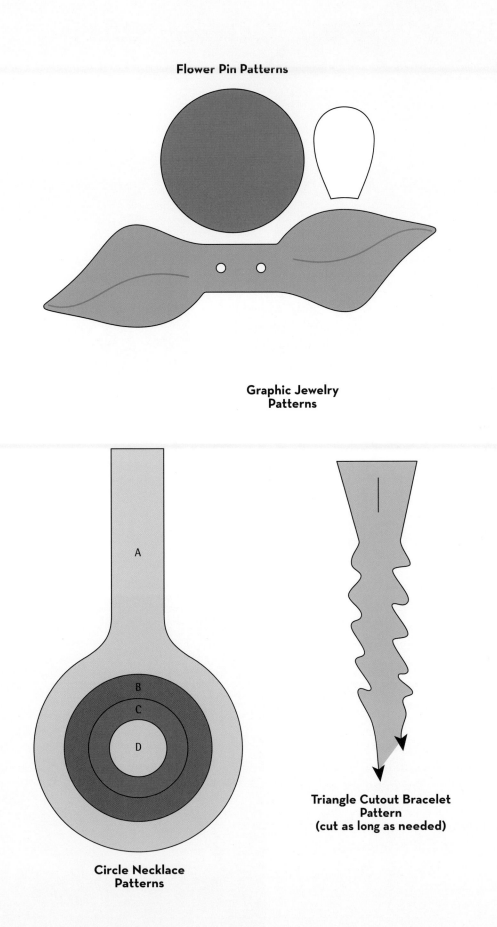

**Graphic Jewelry
Patterns**

A

B
C
D

I

**Circle Necklace
Patterns**

**Triangle Cutout Bracelet
Pattern
(cut as long as needed)**

**Talk With
Your Kids**

Just for
fun, let
everyone
share his
or her
favorite
color
combination
and see if
he or she
has clothes
in those
colors.

Child's-Play Jackets

SUPPLIES
*Child's artwork of several
    colorful designs and motifs
Transfer paper for color fabric,
    such as Hewlett Packard
Color photocopier; scissors
Tracing paper and pencil
    (for adult jacket)
Denim jacket; iron
Acrylic paint in bright colors
Disposable plate
Fabric-painting medium
¼-inch flat paintbrush*

136

SHOW OFF YOUR CHILD'S ARTISTIC ENDEAVORS ON A HIP DENIM JACKET! USE PHOTOCOPIES OF THE ARTWORK JUST AS IT IS, OR CUT IT INTO SHAPES TO MAKE A VIVID SUNRISE DESIGN.

WHAT TO DO

1 Photocopy child's artwork onto transfer paper using setting for color and appropriate paper.

2 For the adult jacket, trace the patterns, *page 139*. Cut out the shapes. To make a small sun design on the jacket front and a large sun design on the back, use patterns to cut a large and a small partial circle, and seven rays of each size from color photocopies.

3 For the child's jacket, cut out several motifs, leaving a ⅛-inch border. Decide on the arrangement of the designs on the jacket.

4 For either jacket, follow the transfer paper manufacturer's instructions to iron the designs where desired on the jacket.

5 Use paint to detail the seams. Place a small amount of paint on the disposable plate. Mix each paint color with fabric painting medium following the manufacturer's instructions.

6 Working on one side at a time, paint seams with solid or dotted lines. Let the paint dry. Turn the jacket over and paint the jacket seams. Let the paint dry.

continued on page 138

Talk With Your Kids

Have every family member choose their favorite season and which jacket they love the most.

137

Child's-Play Jackets continued

Bright Idea
• • • • •
Outline the iron-on designs with fabric paint.

Adult Jacket Front Sunrise Patterns

Jacket details of front, *above,* **and back,** *right*

138

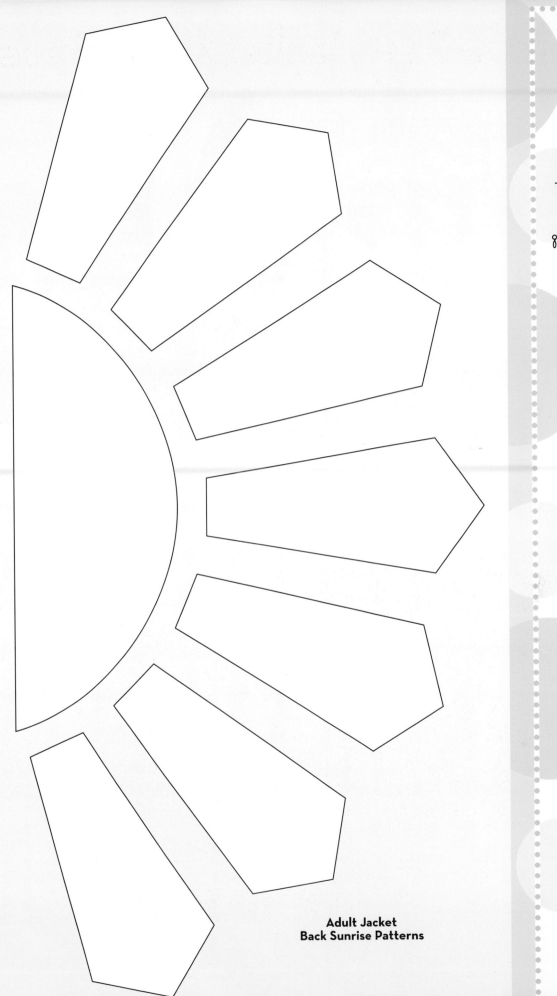

**Adult Jacket
Back Sunrise Patterns**

Talk With Your Kids

Take them to an art gallery and discuss what you saw over lunch.

Celebrate the Holidays

Whether you want to carve a pumpkin,
lay out a scrapbook page, or trim the niftiest holiday
tree ever, this chapter inspires you and your family to
create festive holiday projects all year long.

Halloween Disguises

Hazel & Broomilda

SUPPLIES

*Tape measure; pencil; newspaper; 70-inch round tablecloth for adult skirt
60-inch round tablecloth for youth skirt*

AFTER PARKING THEIR BROOMS AT THE DOOR, THESE WITTY WITCHES ARE READY FOR SOME PARTY BREW. WITH SUCH EASY-TO-MAKE SKIRTS AND CAPES, YOU CAN TRANSFORM INTO A WITCH IN THE BLINK OF A CAT'S EYE.

Fusible hem tape; iron; scissors; elastic
1 yard of black fabric or round tablecloth*
Interfacing; pinking shears; ribbon; button
Purchased shirts and hats

WHAT TO DO

1 For each skirt, measure the waist of the person who will wear the costume. Make a newspaper circle pattern the same circumference as the waist measurement. Cut this circle out of the tablecloth center as shown in the diagram, *below.*

2 Use fusible hem tape to press under 1 inch of raw edge at waist, clipping as necessary to make pressing easy. Make small slits in waistline hem about 1½ inches apart. Thread elastic through the slits; adjust to fit waist.

3 For each cape, measure from the back of the neck downward to determine the cape length. Fold black fabric in half so that center back of cape is on the fold. Draw curve for one-quarter of circle to front edge as shown in diagram, *below.* Cut out a circle for neck. Open cape fabric.

4 Fuse interfacing to fabric around neck edge about 2 inches wide. Trim neck and bottom edges with pinking shears. Fringe the bottom edge with straight-edge scissors.

5 Make ½-inch slits approximately 1 inch apart in neck facing. Thread ribbon through slits, ending with ribbon on the right side. Gather slightly. Sew a button on ribbon through cape to secure gathers. Don purchased hats and shirts.

*Note: Look in the linen department for tablecloths, flat panel curtains, sheets, or shower curtains. When making a cape from flat curtain panel, cut with the front edge on the hem by folding the panel crosswise. Shower curtains and sheets provide large widths of fabric without seams. Round tablecloths make one skirt or two capes.

continued on page 144

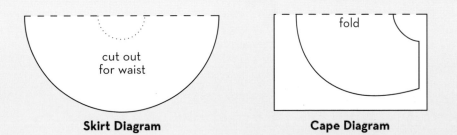

Skirt Diagram   cut out for waist

Cape Diagram   fold

Whoa Nelly Nurse

SUPPLIES

Measuring tape; newspaper; scissors; round white tablecloth
Fusible hem tape; iron; elastic; 60-inch square of white fabric; interfacing
Needle; thread in red and white; pinking shears
Red sequin trim; two 6-inch squares of red fabric; ribbon; button
Wig, hat, hot-water bottle, stethoscope, white stockings and shoes

WHAT TO DO

1 For skirt, measure waist. Make a newspaper circle pattern the circumference of the measurement. Cut out circle from tablecloth center.

2 Use fusible hem tape to press under 1 inch of raw edge at waist, clipping as necessary to make pressing easy. Make small slits in waistline hem about 1½ inches apart. Thread elastic through the slits; adjust to fit waist.

3 For cape, measure from the back of the neck downward to determine the length. Fold white fabric in half so center back of cape is on fold. Draw curve for one-quarter of circle to front edge. Cut out a circle for neck. Open cape fabric.

4 Fuse interfacing to fabric around neck edge about 2 inches wide. Hem center front along selvage. Pink lower edge. Stitch red sequin trim close to outer edge. To make two red crosses, cut out 2-inch squares from each corner of red fabric pieces. Fuse red fabric crosses at lower front corners of cape.

5 Make ½-inch slits approximately 1 inch apart in neck facing. Thread ribbon through slits, ending with ribbon on the right side. Gather slightly. Sew a button on ribbon through cape to secure gathers.

TRICK EVERYONE WITH LONG GOLDEN LOCKS, FLASHY EYEGLASSES, AND BRIGHT LIPSTICK.

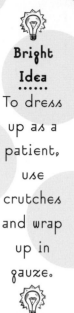

Bright Idea

To dress up as a patient, use crutches and wrap up in gauze.

BRING BACK A LITTLE PIECE OF HISTORY WITH THIS COMFY COSTUME FOR GALS OF ANY AGE.

Talk With Your Kids

Discuss Betsy Ross and the part she played in our history.

Betsy Ross

SUPPLIES

60×89-inch blue check oval tablecloth; scissors; thread; needle
Fusible hem tape; iron; elastic; 20-inch-diameter circle of light blue fabric
Gathered lace; 45-inch square of red calico or purchased afghan
Purchased blouse, sewing basket, embroidery hoop, and star fabric

WHAT TO DO

1 For the skirt, cut the tablecloth lengthwise, 1 inch longer than desired length. Overlap the skirt at front for closure. Baste along the top edge.

2 Use fusible tape to press under 1 inch of raw edge along the top edge of the waist. Cut slits every 2 inches and thread elastic through slits. Adjust to fit waist and tie ends.

3 For the bonnet, stitch lace around outside edge of light blue fabric. Stitch elastic 2 inches in from outer edge.

4 For the shawl, use red calico fabric or a purchased afghan.

cutting line

Skirt Diagram

Bright Idea

Cut out extra foam stars to place on the table around the pumpkin.

Pumpkin with Pizzazz

SUPPLIES

Pumpkin; thick white crafts glue; paintbrush; glitter
Tracing paper; pencil; scissors; crafts foam in desired colors
Hole punch; metallic chenille stems

WHAT TO DO

1 To stick glitter to the pumpkin, use a paintbrush or your fingertip to create glue designs. Do two or three designs at a time and sprinkle with two colors of glitter. Continue making glitter designs all over your pumpkin.

2 To make the foam decorations, trace the desired patterns, *opposite.* Cut out the shapes. Trace around the shapes on foam. Cut out.

3 Glue the pieces in place. Let dry. Squeeze glue where glitter is desired. Sprinkle glitter on glue; let dry. Shake off excess glitter.

4 Using a hole punch, make a hole at the top of each foam piece. Push a chenille stem through each hole and twist to secure. Wrap chenille stems around a pencil to curl. Wrap the loose ends around pumpkin stem.

THESE SPARKLING PUMPKINS SHINE
AMONG YOUR JACK-O'-LANTERNS, AND THEY
LAST LONGER TOO!

**Pumpkin with Pizzazz
Patterns**

**Talk With
Your Kids**
Discuss
easy ways
to "haunt
up" the
house.

Stamped Papers

SUPPLIES

Green bendable polymer clay, such as Sculpey
Bake & Bend; baking sheet; foil
Small piece of thin cardboard
Assorted wood blocks
Crafts glue, such as Fast Grab Tacky Glue
White wrapping paper; newspapers
Frosted glass finishing spray, such as Krylon, in green
and red; spray paints in metallic gold and copper
2 large sheets of crafts foam; crafts sponge
Acrylic paints in red, green, and metallic gold; paper towels
Matte finishing spray; scissors; card stock in red, green, white, and
brushed gold; double-sided tape; metallic gold leafing pen
1/8-inch hole punch; gold eyelets; eyelet tool; ribbon as desired

WHAT TO DO

1 To make stamps, knead and warm clay with hands. Using the shapes as shown in the photos and patterns, *above* and *opposite*, roll clay into long thin ropes; shape clay.

2 Lay shapes right side down on baking sheet lined with foil. Using a thin piece of cardboard, cover each shape one at a time and gently press evenly on the back of the shape to form an even stamping surface.

LET THE KIDS GET IN ON THE JOY OF
WRAPPING PRESENTS BY MAKING THE
GIFT WRAP AND TAGS!

3 Bake clay as directed by the manufacturer; let cool. Glue shapes right side down to wood blocks; let dry overnight.

4 To make wrapping paper, lay paper flat over a newspaper-covered work surface, securing the corners of paper with heavy objects. Alternate spraying green and red frosted glass finishing sprays. Or alternate spraying metallic gold spray with copper spray. Let dry.

5 To stamp images, lay two sheets of crafts foam under the section of wrapping paper to be stamped. Moisten stamp shape with a crafts sponge saturated with acrylic paint. Stamp image on paper and remoisten stamp with paint for each stamping. Wipe stamp clean with a wet paper towel when changing colors or after use. When dry, apply two coats of matte finish.

6 To make tags, cut out card stock shapes using the pattern *below* if desired. Cut and apply pieces of wrapping paper using double-sided tape. Attach a second layer of card stock trimmed with a gold leafing pen. Punch a hole in the top of tags. Attach gold eyelets to the holes using an eyelet tool. Finish with ribbon ties and bows.

Stamped Papers Patterns

Bright Idea
• • • • • •
Tie fine thread to the angels to make them into tree ornaments.

Feather Angels

THESE SOFT FEATHER ANGELS ARE HEAVENLY TO CRAFT!

SUPPLIES

Scissors; paper cone cup (from bottled-water company)
White glue; feathers; chenille stem; pencil; large bead; tape

WHAT TO DO

1 Use scissors to cut off the tip of the cone. Spread glue on half of the outside of the cone. Choose feathers that look pretty together. Place the feathers on the glue with the wide ends pointing downward. When the first half is done, cover the other half of the cone with glue and feathers.

2 For wings, glue large feathers on the back. Wrap one end of the chenille stem tightly around a pencil four times. Remove it from the pencil. Push the straight end of the chenille stem through the bead down to where it curls. Push the chenille stem into the tip of the cone. Tape the stem in place on the inside of the cone.

Merry Macaroni Ornaments

STRING PAINTED PASTA AND BEADS TO MAKE PRETTY TRIMS.

♡
**Talk With
Your Kids**
Think about what your family loves to do most and decorate a tree with that theme.
♡

SUPPLIES

Pasta with holes; disposable plate
Acrylic paints in your favorite colors; paintbrushes; beads; chenille stems

WHAT TO DO

1 Place the pasta on a plate and paint many pieces at a time. Let the paint dry.

2 String beads and pasta onto the middle of the chenille stems. Leave a space at each end. Twist the ends together and form a hanger to place on the tree.

151

USE YOUR FAVORITE COLOR COMBINATIONS TO MAKE A BRILLIANT SET OF MINIATURE TREES TO PARADE AROUND YOUR HOLIDAY HOME.

SUPPLIES

1½-inch terra-cotta flowerpots
Acrylic paints in pink, orange, purple, blue, green, yellow, and white; paintbrushes
Pinecones
Wood stars
Paper napkins
Thick white crafts glue

Pinecone Pots

WHAT TO DO

1 Paint the flowerpots a solid color. Let the paint dry. Choose another color to make stripes or dots. Use a tiny paintbrush to make stripes. Rinse out the paint from the brush well before changing colors.

2 To make dots, dip the handle of a paintbrush into paint and dot onto the outside of the pot. Let dry.

3 Paint the pinecones white. Let dry. Paint them a second time if you need to so pinecones are entirely white. Let the paint dry.

4 Paint the stars to match their pots, using the same paint colors. Let dry. Make little dots or stripes on the stars. Let dry.

5 Fill the pots with pieces of crumpled paper napkins to prop up the pinecones. Then put a generous amount of glue on the crumpled napkins. Set the pinecones onto the wet napkins and glue the stars onto the pinecones.

Bright Idea
• • • • •
Paint names on the stars and use them as place cards.

Feather Candles

SUPPLIES

Cardboard tube from toilet paper or paper towels; colored paper
Pencil; scissors; glue stick; glitter paint; round jar lid
Acrylic paints; paintbrush; thick white crafts glue
Beads and jewels; orange or yellow feather

WHAT TO DO

1 To make the colored paper the right size to cover the cardboard tube, lay the tube on the paper and draw a pencil line at the top of the tube. Roll the paper around the tube and mark another line where you need to cut it. Cut out the colored paper along the pencil lines.

2 Rub a glue stick over the back side of the paper and roll it around the tube.

3 Apply glitter paint along the top edge of candle. Apply extra paint to make drips.

4 Paint the lid the color you wish. Let paint dry.

5 Use dots of glue to adhere the candle into the bottom of the lid. Put a puddle of glitter paint into the lid around the candle. Press beads and jewels into the wet glitter.

6 Cut a point on the end of the feather to make it look like a flame. Glue the feather to the inside of the tube.

FEATHERS MAKE A SAFE FLAME FOR THESE COLORFUL CANDLES DRIPPING WITH GLITTER PAINT AND JEWELS.

Winter Wonders

Bright Idea
·····
Use paper cutouts to make winter note cards.

SUPPLIES

Crafts foam sheets
Decorative-edge scissors; crafts foam cutouts
Small foam rollers 2 to 3 inches wide
Hot-glue gun and glue sticks
Tracing paper; pencil
Construction paper; acrylic paints in colors you like
Disposable plates; paper towels
Pom-poms; scissors; string
Miniature clothespins

WHAT TO DO

1 To prepare the rollers, cut foam strips with decorative-edge scissors. Hot-glue them, along with the purchased cutouts, around the rollers.

2 Trace the mitten and hat patterns, *pages 156–157*, onto the foam or construction paper. Wait to cut them out because it is easier to print on full sheets.

3 Print lighter colors on darker backgrounds and darker colors on lighter backgrounds. Squeeze paint onto a disposable plate and roll the foam roller in the paint until the foam is completely covered. The trick to printing with a roller is to make a line without picking up the roller. Practice on construction paper before printing on the mitten and hat

STRING UP A CLOTHESLINE FULL OF HATS AND MITTENS
TO WELCOME YOUR GUESTS IN OUT OF THE COLD.

shapes. Wash out the roller to switch colors and squeeze out extra water carefully with a paper towel.

4 Pinch the pom-poms between your thumb and first finger, dip them into the paint. Print dots directly onto the hat and mittens. Let dry.

5 Cut out the hats and mittens. Use miniature clothespins to hang them on a string clothesline.

continued on page 156

155

Talk With Your Kids

Discuss what you think winter might be like in another part of the world.

Winter Wonders continued

Bright Idea

Use the mitten pattern to cut shapes from felt. Embellish the shape with simple stitches and glue pom-poms on the cuff for easy gift trims and tree ornaments.

Mitten Pattern

Hat Pattern

Talk With Your Kids

Have the kids think of someone with a winter birthday. Ask the kids to make that person a card using the hat pattern.

157

Bright Idea
· · · · · ·
To make edible trees, thread three sizes of green gumdrops on a pretzel stick. Plant the tree in a large gumdrop of another color to hold it upright.

Happy Holiday Houses

WANT TO DISH UP SOME HOLIDAY EXCITEMENT? SAVE MILK AND JUICE CARTONS, THEN HEAD FOR THE KITCHEN!

SUPPLIES

Small milk or juice cartons, clean and dry; masking tape
Meringue powder (available in crafts and cake-decorating stores)
Confectioner's sugar; mixing bowl
Electric mixer; food coloring
Pastry bag and tip
Spoon; knife; graham crackers
Assorted candies, cookies, sugar sprinkles, and cake-decorating candies

WHAT TO DO

1 Tape the carton opening closed. Make the frosting following instructions for Royal Icing on the meringue powder package. Tint the frosting with food coloring if desired. Spoon frosting into pastry bag.

2 Snap apart crackers to cover the carton sides and form the roof. For ease in breaking, score the crackers with a knife; snap them apart. *Note:* Crackers will not meet in the corners, as shown in the top two photos, *right*. Score and snap cracker squares on the diagonal for peaked front and back.

3 Use frosting to hold the pieces to the carton. Let dry overnight for easier handling.

4 Referring to the photos, *right* and *opposite*, frost the entire house or fill the corners and frost only the roof; press cookies and andies in place for decoration.

Talk With Your Kids

Discuss the importance of washing your hands before you head to the kitchen to make food or eat.

159

Away in a Manger

Bright Idea
Create a manger by cutting an opening in a birdhouse.

Animals great and small played important roles in the Christmas story. Here are four fuzzy creatures to make for play or display.

SUPPLIES

Tracing paper; pencil; scissors

Thread and needle; ⅔ yard of straw-pattern and straw-color cotton fabric (for backing and base); straight pins; sewing machine

Recycled wool from old blankets, sweaters, or other clothing; good-quality wool felt (see specifics below); polyester fiberfill; quilting thread

Hot-glue gun and glue sticks; ½ yard of straw-color upholstery fringe

5-inch doll needle; small white buttons for eyes

FOR THE CAMEL: *Wool fabric felt in gold and red; embroidered trim Green pom-poms; red and white rope trim; black elastic cording*

FOR THE DONKEY: *Wool in black and white herringbone and dark gray Jute rope; red and white cording*

FOR THE COW: *Wool felt in brown and pink; jute rope*

FOR THE LAMB: *White wool; black wool felt*

continued on page 162

Talk With Your Kids
Read the Christmas story together.

Away in a Manger continued

Bright Idea

Make extra animals to tuck in the branches of the holiday tree and for little ones to play with.

WHAT TO DO

1 For all animals, enlarge and trace the patterns, *opposite*. Cut out the shapes. Cut two 20-inch squares and one oval base from cotton fabric for each animal. Center and trace animal shape on right side of one fabric square. Cut body parts from appropriate fabrics; then pin to the fabric square. Using a zigzag stitch, machine-appliqué around each piece.

2 With right sides facing, pin the appliquéd front to the remaining square. Using zigzag stitching as a guide, sew around the design, leaving the bottom open. Trim seam allowance to ½ inch; clip curves.

3 Pin the base to the opening with right sides facing. Sew around the base, leaving an opening for turning. Trim seam allowances and clip curves. Turn animal right side out; stuff with fiberfill. Sew opening closed.

4 Hand-quilt the animal, especially along the legs and body. Hot-glue fringe around bottom edge to represent straw.

FOR THE CAMEL

1 Cut out a blanket from red felt; then attach trims. Glue blanket and pom-poms to the camel.

2 Roll a 3×5-inch piece of gold felt into a tube for the tail. Cut fringe at one end. Hand-stitch the tail to secure it. Sew the tail to the seam.

3 Cut out the ears and sew them to the head. Sew the button eyes in place. Trim elastic cording for the bridle pieces and glue them in place, referring to the photo on *page 161*.

FOR THE DONKEY

1 Make the tail as instructed for the camel. For ears, zigzag-stitch the herringbone fabric in the shape of the ear pattern. Cut out the ears, fold them in half lengthwise, and sew to the head.

2 Unravel jute for the mane, glue along the neck seam, and trim. Sew on button eyes. Adhere cording for bridle, referring to photo on *page 163*.

FOR THE COW

1 Trace head pattern onto brown felt. Appliqué a pink muzzle. Pin head to a second piece of brown felt; zigzag around head, placing fiberfill between the layers. Cut out head, sew on eyes, and glue head to body.

2 Make the tail as for camel. Zigzag pink and brown felt together in an ear shape. Cut out, fold, and attach ears. Glue jute between them.

FOR THE LAMB

1 Sew tail pieces together, leaving straight edge open. Trim seam, clip curve, and turn. Turn under the seam allowance at opening; glue tail to the seam line.

2 Cut the ears and head from black felt; attach button eyes. Glue the ears and head to the body.

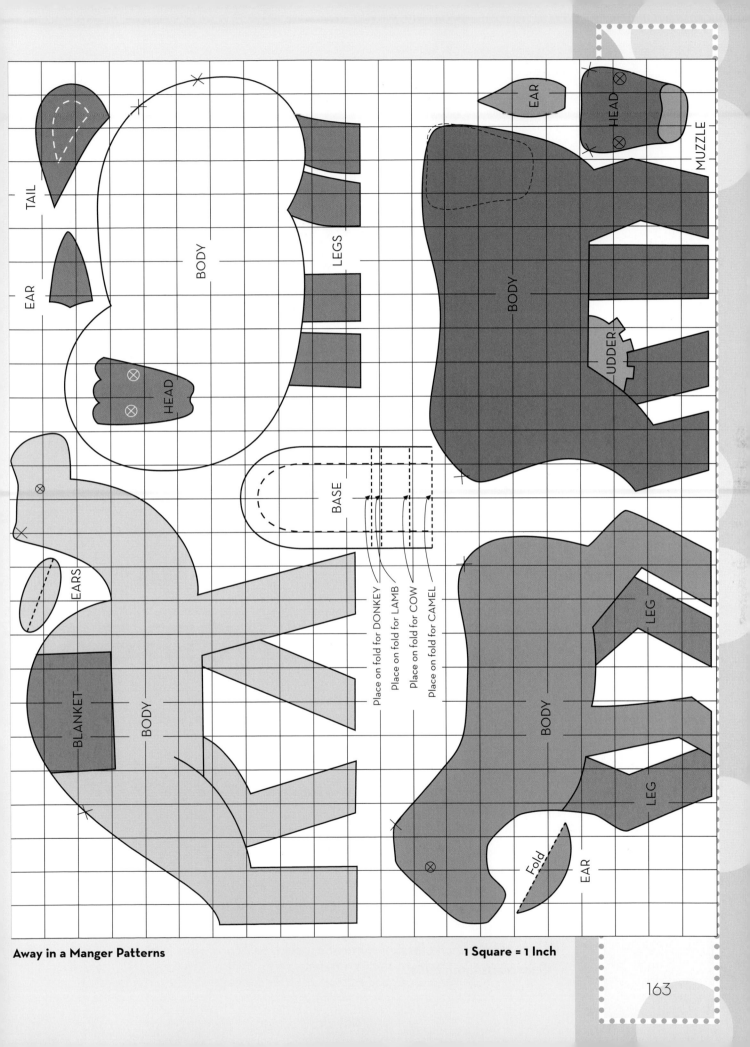

TAIL

EAR

BODY

LEGS

HEAD

EAR

HEAD

MUZZLE

BODY

UDDER

BASE

Place on fold for DONKEY
Place on fold for LAMB
Place on fold for COW
Place on fold for CAMEL

EARS

BLANKET

BODY

LEG

BODY

LEG

Fold

EAR

Away in a Manger Patterns

1 Square = 1 Inch

Bright Idea
......
String gumdrops on dental floss to make bright garland.

Candy Christmas

Gumdrop Trees

SUPPLIES
Three 4-inch-diameter wood disks for bases
Drill and 1⅛-inch drill bit
Acrylic paints in red, yellow, and green
Paintbrush
Acrylic matte medium
Sugar; 7 peppermint sticks
Masking tape; hot-glue gun and glue sticks
Sharp knife
6-, 9-, and 12-inch plastic-foam cones, such as Styrofoam
Gumdrops; gum balls

CHRISTMAS CRAFTING IS SUCH A TREAT, ESPECIALLY WHEN YOU USE SWEETS.

WHAT TO DO

1 For the tree with peppermint trunk, drill a 1⅛-inch-diameter hole partway through center of one wood disk. Paint disks for bases; let dry. Coat bases with acrylic matte medium and dust heavily with sugar. Let dry. Shake off excess.

2 Hold peppermint sticks in a bundle; tape together at one end. Glue untaped end in the base. Cut a hole in bottom of small cone. Insert trunk; glue in place.

3 Glue gumdrops to cones. Top each tree with a gum ball. Glue solid gumdrop trees directly to the bases.

Candy Cornucopia

SUPPLIES

Low-temp glue gun and glue sticks
⅓ yard of ribbon; sugar or waffle cone
Meringue powder (available in crafts and cake-decorating stores)
Mixing bowl; electric mixer
Confectioner's sugar
Spoon; pastry bag and tip; candies

WHAT TO DO

1 Glue ribbon ends to the inside of the cone for a hanger. Following instructions for Royal Icing on the meringue powder package, make frosting; spoon it into a pastry bag. Pipe frosting around the cone top and along the seam; press candies into frosting for decoration.

continued on page 166

Bright Idea
······
Arrange light catchers along a mantel and back them with tea lights for a pretty display.

Sweet Light Catchers

SUPPLIES
Metal cookie cutters
Aluminum foil; baking sheet; nonstick cooking spray
Translucent hard candies
Small heavy-duty resealable plastic bags
Kitchen towel; hammer; toothpick

WHAT TO DO

1 Preheat oven to 325°. Place cookie cutters on foil-lined baking sheet. For ornaments, coat inside the cutters with cooking spray so candy can be removed easily after baking.

2 Separate candies by color and place like colors in plastic bags; seal. Cover with a kitchen towel and coarsely crush candies using a hammer. Spoon crushed candies into cookie cutters, forming a ¼-inch-thick layer. Bake 4 minutes or until candies begin to melt. Avoid overbaking. Let cool; remove from foil. For ornaments, cool baked candies 2 minutes; use a toothpick to make a hole for hanging loop. Leave candy shapes in cookie cutters for light catchers or ornaments if desired.

Twinkle, Twinkle, Licorice Stars

SUPPLIES

Licorice sticks in any flavor
Scissors; ruler
Thin wire
Small candies with holes in
*   the centers*

WHAT TO DO

1 Trim ends from licorice. Cut into five 3½-inch-long pieces for small stars or 4½-inch pieces for large stars.

2 Thread wire through center hole of licorice and insert a candy; repeat four more times. Referring to the photo, *right*, shape wire into a star shape, weaving pieces over and under each other. Twist the wire ends together.

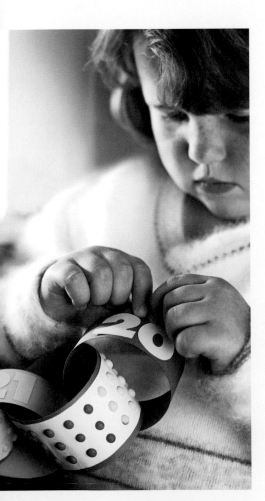

Countdown Garland

SUPPLIES

Double-sided tape; 5 paper strips of
*   candy dots; scissors; 12-inch card stock*
*   squares in pink, lime, purple, and blue*
Ruler; yellow paper numbers; glue

WHAT TO DO

1 Tape each candy-dots strip to pink card stock and cut out, leaving a narrow border. Tape ends together to form a ring.

2 Cut twenty-five 1½×11½-inch strips from lime, purple, and blue card stock. Join rings, alternating candy and plain rings. Glue numbers to plain rings.

continued on page 168

Talk With
Your Kids
Talk about when candy is safe to eat. If it has been used for decorating, do not eat it.

**Bright
Idea**
......
Carry out
the candy
theme in
your
holiday
home by
hanging
wrapped
candy
canes on
the tree.

Candy Christmas continued

Candyland Swirls

SUPPLIES

24-ounce box of ready-to-use white fondant
  (available in grocery and crafts stores; makes
  8 lollipops or one large tree and one lollipop)
Paste food coloring in green, pink, and purple
Ruler; plastic wrap; 8-inch lollipop sticks; knife
Low-temp glue gun and glue sticks
8- to 10-inch-tall plastic-foam cone, such as
  Styrofoam; hard candies

WHAT TO DO

1 Cut off one-fourth of the fondant. (Be prepared to work quickly to prevent fondant from drying out.) Knead in food coloring; shape into an 8-inch-long log. Set aside. Cut remaining white fondant in half. Shape each half into an 8-inch-long log.

2 Cut all three logs in half lengthwise, making six logs. Place a colored log between two white logs; press together to form one larger log. Holding the end, twist pieces to swirl the colors. Repeat with remaining logs.

3 Working with one twisted log at a time, roll the fondant on a large, flat surface to create a rope about 36 inches long. Cut rope in half and continue to twist and roll each rope piece to 36 inches. After twisting and rolling the fondant, you should have four 36-inch ropes, each about ½ inch in diameter. Keep ropes covered with plastic wrap until ready to use.

4 For lollipop, shape one rope into a triangle or circle, beginning in the center. Moisten ends with water; press in place to seal the shape. Insert stick. Let dry 1 hour.

5 For tree, apply glue to bottom 2 inches of cone. Wrap rope around cone. Continue to glue and wrap until cone is covered. Let it dry 1 hour. Glue candy to top.

Goody, Goody, Gumdrops Garland

SUPPLIES
3-ounce bathroom paper cup; card stock in assorted colors; pencil Scissors; gumdrops; needle; heavy-duty thread

WHAT TO DO

1 Using cup, trace circles onto card stock; cut out. String circles and gumdrops onto heavy-duty thread.

Talk With Your Kids
Look online or in books to find out about various kinds of evergreens.

Make a scrapbook all about Christmas!
It's a great project to do during holiday break
and one to anticipate each year.

A Merry Scrapbook

Christmas (OPPOSITE)

Organization is the key to this page. Here are some tips to get you started:

- Tear paper to create an interesting edge on background paper.
- Use a purchased tag for each family member.
- Choose stickers to emphasize the theme.
- Crop several photos the same size and arrange in a grid formation.

Tonight (ABOVE)

Make a sentimental page like this one in the wink of an eye. Here's how:

- Incorporate a handwritten letter to Santa.
- Secure some of the papers using eyelets.
- Create a headline and journaling on a computer.
- Tear and chalk edges for vintage appeal.

Talk With Your Kids

Discuss the history of jolly ol' St. Nick.

171

PUT UP A TREE, HANG THE TRIMS, AND YOU'RE READY FOR CHRISTMAS! THIS YEAR, SPREAD THE EXCITEMENT TO YOUR OWN ROOM. HERE ARE A PAIR OF HOLIDAY TREES DESIGNED ESPECIALLY FOR YOU.

A Tree in My Room

Bright Idea
Purchase Christmas lights in fun colors, such as purple or pink, and use for birthday parties.

Too-Cool Shades

SUPPLIES

Tracing paper
Pencil; scissors
Scrapbook paper
Transparent pink plastic
Tape; 1-inch-diameter
  pink paper flower stickers
  (available in scrapbook stores)

WHAT TO DO

1 Trace pattern, *page 177*, onto tracing paper; make a mirror image along center line. Cut out the shape. Trace shape onto scrapbook paper and cut out.

2 From the transparent plastic, cut ovals to fit behind the openings. Tape the ovals in place. Fold sunglasses as noted on the pattern. Decorate with paper flowers.

Talk With Your Kids
....
Talk about good cell phone manners.

"Call Me!" Cellular Phone

SUPPLIES

Tracing paper
Pencil
Scissors
Crafts foam in pink, teal, lime, and purple
Foam adhesive; sharp pencil
Coated round pastel brads (available in scrapbook stores)
Ultrathin $5/8$-inch flower button (available in scrapbook stores)

WHAT TO DO

1 Trace the patterns on *page 176* onto tracing paper and cut out. Trace the shapes onto crafts foam and cut out.

2 Glue the teal rectangle to the pink cell phone. Use a sharp pencil to poke holes for the phone buttons. Push a brad through each hole. Open the prongs on the back of the phone.

3 Glue the lime rectangle and purple circle in place. Glue a button to the purple circle.

continued on page 174

"Got a Size 4?" Mary Janes

SUPPLIES

Tracing paper; pencil; scissors
Crafts foam in pink, teal, lime, and purple;
 scrapbook papers in assorted patterns
Foam adhesive; 1/16-inch hole punch
Round pastel brads (available at
 scrapbook stores)
1¼-inch-diameter bright pink
 self-adhesive flowers
1-inch-diameter pink paper flowers (available at scrapbook stores)

WHAT TO DO

1 Trace patterns, *pages 176–177,* onto tracing paper; cut out shapes. Trace one sole onto crafts foam and another onto scrapbook paper for lining. Trace two heels onto one color of foam and three heels onto another color. Trace shoe strap and shoe upper onto scrapbook paper, placing shoe upper on fold of paper at the broken line. Cut out all shapes. Clip narrow, even slits all around the shoe upper as noted on pattern. Bend under slits.

2 Matching Xs, glue the shoe upper to the foam sole, working from center front to back of shoe. Overlap excess paper at back and glue. Stack and glue five heels together, alternating colors. Glue stacked heels to sole.

3 Slip lining into shoe; trim it to fit. Punch holes in shoe upper and strap as noted on patterns. Align holes; secure with brads. Adhere the flowers.

Fancy Wrap-Ups

SUPPLIES

Tracing paper; pencil; scissors
Crafts foam in pink, teal, lime, and purple
Round metal brads (available in scrapbook stores); scissors

WHAT TO DO

1 Trace the pattern, *page 176,* onto tracing paper, making a mirror image along the center line; cut it out. Enlarge the pattern 150 percent to make a tree topper. Cut the shape from foam.

2 Use a pencil to poke holes through foam as marked by dots on pattern. Fold holes on square tabs to meet the center hole. Push brad through holes; open prongs on back.

Bright Idea
......
Make these cute shoes for party favors and fill them with wrapped candies.

"How Do I Look?" Mirror Ornaments

SUPPLIES

Tracing paper; pencil; ruler; scissors
Crafts foam in pink, teal, lime, and purple
Decorative-edge scissors; pinking shears; foam adhesive
1-inch- and 3-inch-square mirrors
½-inch-wide sheer pink wire-edge ribbon

WHAT TO DO

1 For small mirror, draw 2½- and 3-inch-squares on tracing paper. For large mirror, draw 3½- and 4-inch-squares. Cut out the squares.

2 For each mirror, cut out one small and one large square, each from a different color of crafts foam. Recut using decorative-edge scissors and pinking shears.

3 Glue mirror to small foam square. Cut two 7-inch lengths of ribbon. Glue one end of each ribbon to the back of small foam square. Glue small and large foam squares together. Tie ribbon ends for a hanging loop.

Handbag Chic

SUPPLIES

Tracing paper; pencil; scissors
Crafts foam in pink, teal, lime, and purple
Ultrathin buttons in ³/₈- and ³/₄-inch squares
* and ⁷/₁₆- and ⁵/₈-inch flowers (available in*
* scrapbook stores); embroidery needle; sewing thread*
Thin wire (for Handbag A)

WHAT TO DO

1 Trace handbag patterns, *pages 178–179,* onto tracing paper; cut out. Cut flaps and cutout sections for Handbags B and C. Trace patterns onto foam. Cut out the shapes.

2 Fold up each handbag as noted on the pattern. Fold down the flap over the front of handbag. Sew buttons to flap through all layers.

3 For Handbag A, thread beads onto wire for the handle. Push the ends through the foam at Xs noted on the pattern; coil the ends to secure.

continued on page 176

Talk With Your Kids
Chat in the kitchen while the kids help with the holiday baking. Think of people who would appreciate a visit and a plate of homemade treats.

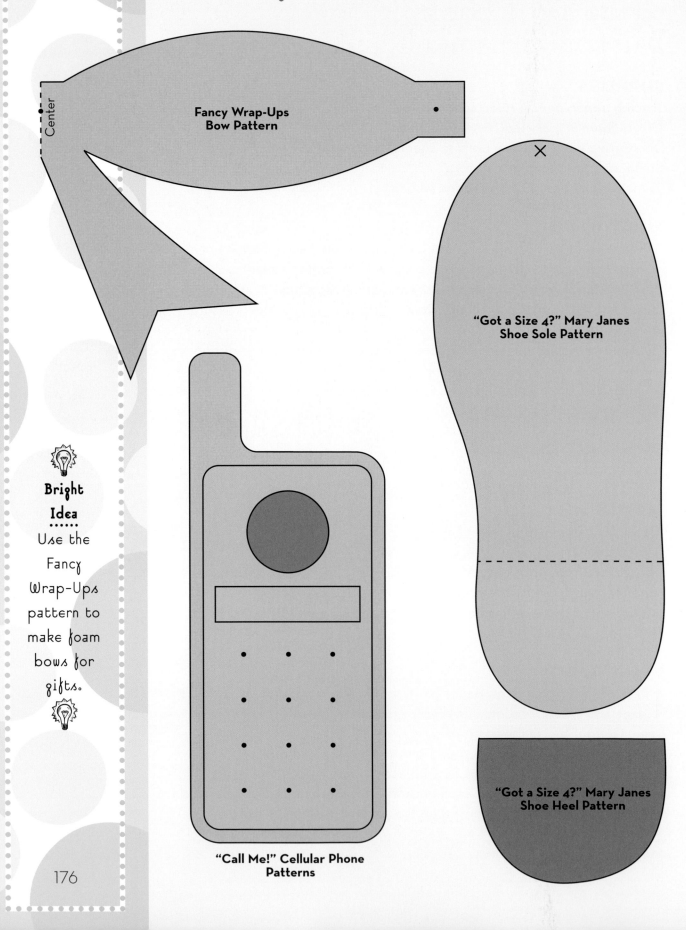

Center

**Fancy Wrap-Ups
Bow Pattern**

×

**"Got a Size 4?" Mary Janes
Shoe Sole Pattern**

**Bright
Idea**
Use the
Fancy
Wrap-Ups
pattern to
make foam
bows for
gifts.

**"Call Me!" Cellular Phone
Patterns**

**"Got a Size 4?" Mary Janes
Shoe Heel Pattern**

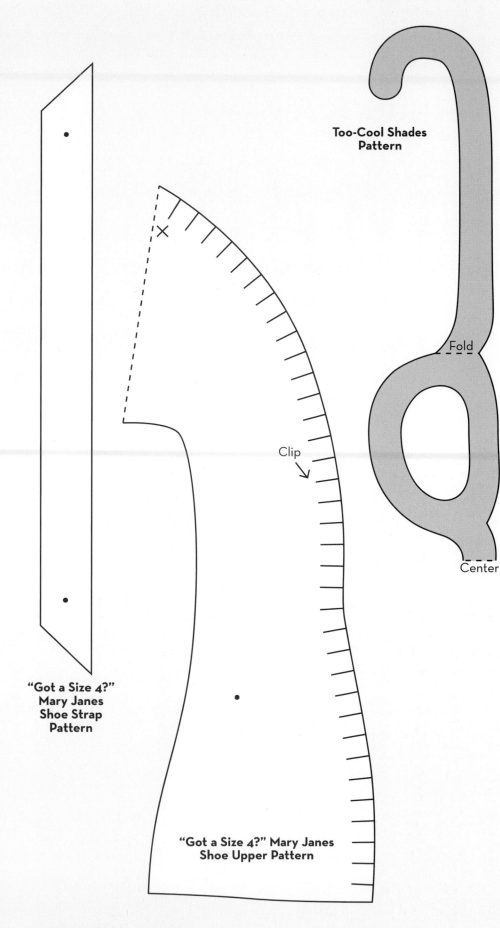

Too-Cool Shades Pattern

Fold

Center

Clip

"Got a Size 4?" Mary Janes Shoe Strap Pattern

"Got a Size 4?" Mary Janes Shoe Upper Pattern

continued on page 178

Talk With Your Kids
Tell them about the holiday tree decorations you had when you were a child.

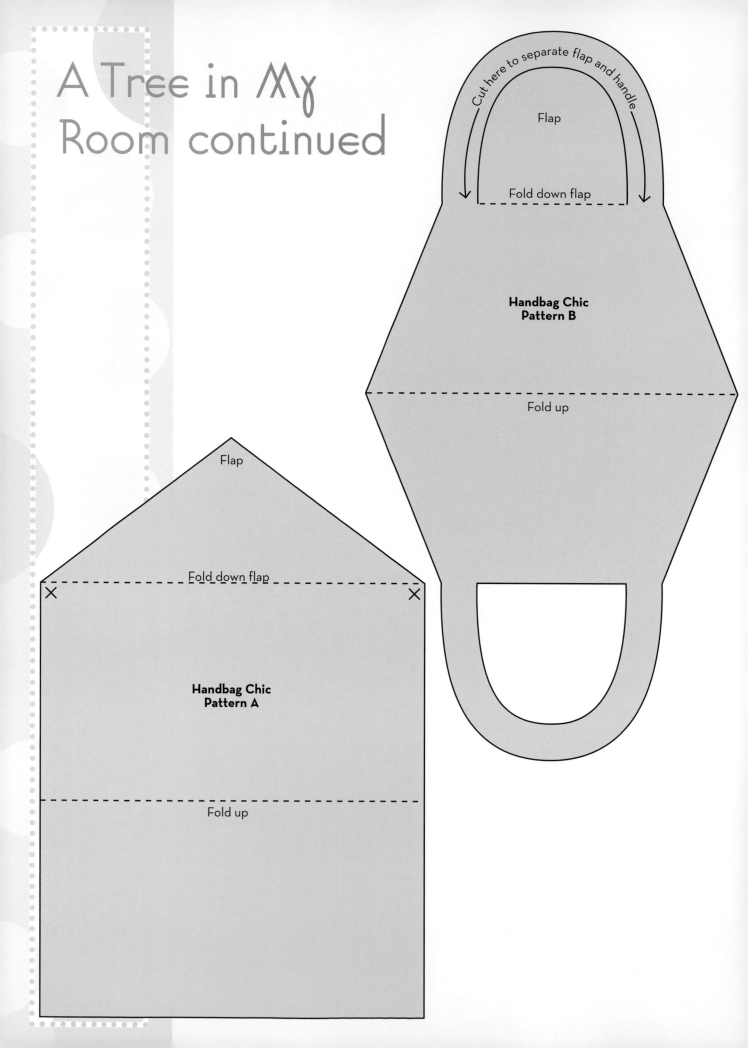

A Tree in My
Room continued

Cut here to separate flap and handle

Flap

Fold down flap

**Handbag Chic
Pattern B**

Fold up

Flap

Fold down flap

×   ×

**Handbag Chic
Pattern A**

Fold up

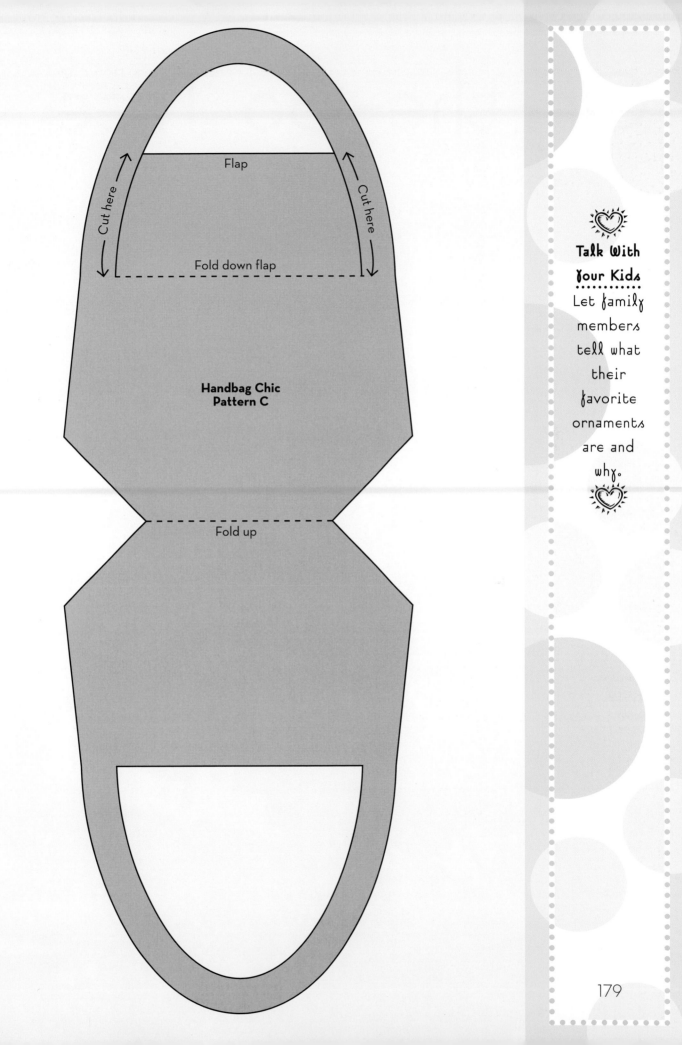

Cut here

Cut here

Flap

Fold down flap

Handbag Chic
Pattern C

Fold up

Talk With
Your Kids
Let family
members
tell what
their
favorite
ornaments
are and
why.

On-the-Go Tree

Bright Idea
......
Let the kids cut out paper circus animals to use as decorations on the train cars.

Talk With
Your Kids
Think up
television-
related
themes you
could
apply to a
Christmas
tree.

"Indy 500 Fun" Garland

SUPPLIES

Tracing paper; pencil; scissors; ruler
Card stock in lime, red, and blue
Black and white check scrapbook paper
Black soutache braid or other thin cording
Pony beads in red, white, and blue; double-sided tape

Place on fold

"Indy 500 Fun"
Garland
Pattern

WHAT TO DO

1 Trace the pattern, *right*, onto tracing paper. Cut out the shape.
Cut card stock and scrapbook paper into 5-inch-wide strips, running
the length of the sheets. Fold each strip in half lengthwise.

2 Trace the pattern on one side, aligning the broken line with the paper
fold. Cut out the flags.

3 Cut 36-inch (or longer) lengths of braid. Knot a small loop in one end
for hanging. Thread a bead onto the braid from the opposite end.
Fold a flag over the braid and tape the tips together; push flag down to
the bead. Keep stringing beads and flags in this way until braid is almost
filled. Tie a loop in the end.

continued on page 182

WHEN LOOKING FOR A TRANSPORTATION THEME
FOR A TREE, THIS ENGINEERED EVERGREEN FINISHES
FIRST! ALL IT TAKES IS PAPER, BEADS, CANDIES, AND A
LITTLE IMAGINATION TO MAKE THIS TREE A HIT.

Holiday Biplane

SUPPLIES

Tracing paper; pencil; scissors
Red card stock; thick white crafts glue
Double-sided tape; 2 sticks of chewing gum
2 rolls of open circular candy, such as Life Savers
Small candy from a candy necklace
Lime chenille stem; ruler

Holiday Biplane Propeller Pattern

WHAT TO DO

1 Trace circle pattern, *right*, onto tracing paper and cut out. Cut circle from red card stock.

2 Referring to the photo, *right*, glue or tape the gum wings to one roll of circular candy. Add red circle propeller and a small candy from candy necklace to the plane front.

3 Open the other roll of circular candy and use two candies for wheels. Cut a 6-inch piece of chenille stem. Wrap ends of stem around candy wheels. Fold stem in half. Glue the fold of stem around front of plane.

Paper-Chain Train

SUPPLIES

Tracing paper; pencil; scissors
Ruler; 12-inch squares of card stock in lime, red, and blue
Thick white crafts glue
Size 1 and size 4 black sew-on snaps
Square and round brads (available in scrapbook stores)
1/8-inch hole punch; 3/16-inch eyelets; eyelet tool
Two 3/4-inch-diameter split rings

Bright Idea
Land a biplane on each Christmas dinner plate.

Talk With Your Kids

Talk about recycling. Instead of tossing out things, such as cardboard tubes and jar lids, think up ways to turn them into holiday trims.

WHAT TO DO

1 Trace patterns, *below*, onto tracing paper; cut out shapes. Cut card stock into 1¼×12-inch strips (one for each train). Fold strips in half, matching short edges. Open strip. Then fold short ends to center. Open strip and refold accordion-style. Trace the car pattern on the folded piece and cut out with scissors. Cut out one smokestack and three squares for each train.

2 Glue a square to the engine and another to the caboose. Fold the remaining square in half diagonally for the cowcatcher. Secure it over the front tab on the engine. Glue a triangle smokestack.

3 Separate the snaps for wheels. Glue one large and three small snaps to the engine. Glue four small snaps to each car. Make windows along the train with brads.

4 Punch a hole in the corner of the engine and caboose. Insert eyelets following package directions. Slip split rings through the eyelets for hanging loops.

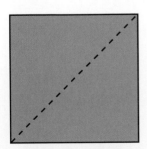

Paper-Chain Train Engine Cab, Caboose Cab, and Cowcatcher Pattern

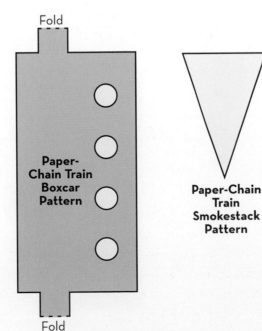

Fold

Paper-Chain Train Boxcar Pattern

Fold

Paper-Chain Train Smokestack Pattern

Pretty Pasta Ornaments

Bright Idea
······
Let the kids make pasta brooches for holiday gifts.

MERRY CHRISTMAS

Colors and shapes and sizes—oh my! These pasta sensations are a pure pleasure to make. Share the idea with your friends!

SUPPLIES

Interesting-shape pasta, such as lasagna, couscous, alphabets, shell, rotini, rigatoni, and spaghetti
Water; bowl; scissors; short drinking straw; paper towels; paintbrushes
Disposable plate
Acrylic paints in desired colors
Thick white crafts glue
Fine string or embroidery floss

WHAT TO DO

1 To make lasagna-backed ornaments, soak the lasagna in a bowl of warm water just long enough to soften it; this makes it easier to cut with scissors without splitting as shown in Photo A, *right*. This takes about 30 to 40 minutes. Avoid soaking too long or lasagna will get mushy. Make a hole with a straw for hanging. Blot excess water with paper towels and allow the lasagna to dry.

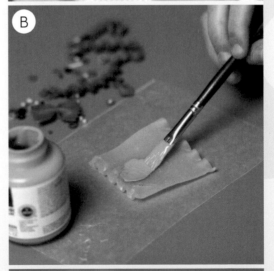

2 Paint pasta pieces in desired colors as shown in Photo B. When painting a large quantity of tiny pieces, such as the couscous or alphabet macaroni, put the pieces on a disposable plate, paint them in a pile, and let them dry as shown in Photo C. Avoid using too much paint.

3 If using lasagna, glue the smaller pieces on it however you wish. For other styles of ornaments, glue the pieces together or string them on fine string or embroidery floss if they have center holes. Allow the trims to dry.

4 Tie a piece of string at the top of each ornament for hanging.

Talk With Your Kids
Have the kids make a list of their favorite pasta and sauce.

185

Donner   Rudolph   Blitzen

Holiday Magic
Blizzard-in-a-Bowl Trail Mix

SUPPLIES

Jumbo and miniature marshmallows; miniature candy-coated chocolates
Candy corn; chocolate chips; pretzel sticks; large bowl
Canned icing (optional)

WHAT TO DO

1 Mix the first five ingredients together in a large bowl. For the snow figures, *below*, put the pieces together using canned icing. Push pretzels into the center marshmallow for arms.

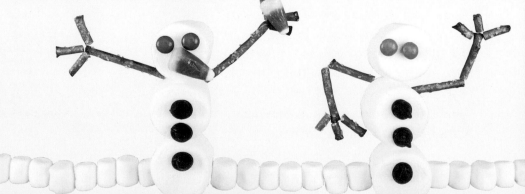

Bright Idea
Display various colors and sizes of jingle bells in pretty clear glass jars.

Jingle All the Way Frame

SUPPLIES

Photo; 10-inch-square frame
1 red and 1 white 15-inch square of terry cloth
Fabric adhesive, such as Beacon's Fabri-Tac; pencil; scissors; tape
Photo; ruler; seven 1-inch-diameter silver jingle bells; needle; thread

WHAT TO DO

1 Place photo in frame. Center frame, right side down, on the wrong side of the red terry cloth. Stretch fabric to back of frame; glue in place.

2 On back of frame, mark an X in the photo opening from corner to corner. Carefully cut the fabric along the X. Glue fabric sections to back of frame, cutting away excess to reduce bulk. Tape the photo in place.

3 For the cuff, cut a 6×12½-inch strip from white terry cloth. Turn under and glue a ½-inch allowance all around. Fold the strip in half lengthwise with wrong sides facing. Glue ½-inch allowances together at the short sides. Hand-sew bells to the front edge of the cuff. Slip the cuff over the frame.

Little "Deers" Greeting Card

SUPPLIES

2 white and 1 brown piece of 8½×11-inch card stock
Scissors; ruler; pencil; eraser; double-sided tape; thick white crafts glue
Wiggly eyes; pom-poms in black and red; black permanent marking pen
9×12-inch catalog envelope and extra postage

WHAT TO DO

1 Fold one piece of white card stock in half lengthwise for the card. Cut a 2×11-inch strip from second piece; make a wavy cut along one long edge for snow.

2 Draw a line horizontally across the center of the brown paper. Lay the paper flat with the long edges at the top and bottom. Place the palm of your hand on the drawn line with your fingertips about 1 inch from the top edge. Trace around your hand above the drawn line only. Repeat across the paper. Erase the lines.

3 Cut along the drawn line to the first hand. Cut around the hand to the next line. Continue cutting across the paper in this way.

4 Tape the shape to the folded card. Glue on snow strip, eyes, and pom-pom noses. Write names and a greeting. Use a catalog envelope with extra postage to mail.

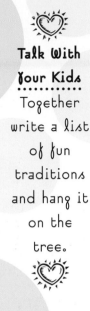

187

Bright Idea
··········
Explain what makes a photo a keeper and then let the kids take turns using the family camera.

Cards of Clay

SUPPLIES
White air-dry clay, such as Crayola Model Magic; rolling pin
Cookie cutter; small beads or jewels; textured papers in red and white
Scissors; thick white crafts glue

WHAT TO DO
1 Use a rolling pin to flatten the white clay until it is about ¼ inch thick. Cut out a shape with a cookie cutter.

2 Before clay dries press beads or jewels into the surface. Push them in firmly without smashing the clay.

3 Cut out shapes from textured papers. Glue the red and white papers together. Glue the clay shape on top. Let the glue dry.

A PINCH OF CLAY AND PRETTY JEWELS MAKE THE COOLEST VALENTINES TO GIVE TO SOMEONE YOU LOVE.

Lots of Love Bag

SUPPLIES

Iron-safe canvas or fabric bag; acrylic paint; paintbrush
Photo; ink-jet fabric sheets, such as Quick Fuse Inkjet Fabric Sheets
Computer with scanner and printer or photocopier
Decorative-edge scissors; thin towel; iron; fabric glue; string of sequins

WHAT TO DO

1 Begin with clean, dry, and pressed bag. Determine where you want areas of soft color. Thin acrylic paint with water to a transparent consistency and brush on simple swashes of color. Let the bag dry.

2 Choose your photo and either use a computer to scan and print the image or a photocopier to copy it. Alter a color photo to black and white if desired. Enlarge it to the size you wish. Print following the fabric sheet manufacturer's instructions. Trim to desired size with decorative-edge scissors.

3 Position trimmed photo on the fabric bag. Place a thin towel over it and iron firmly according to fabric sheet instructions.

4 Use fabric glue to draw a line onto bag where you want sequins. Press sequins onto glue and let dry.

PERSONALIZE A FABRIC TOTE OR GIFT BAG USING THIS EASY PHOTO TRANSFER METHOD.

Talk With Your Kids

Ask the children why they think a heart shape means love.

Blooming Valentine Pots

Bright Idea
• • • • •
For a weather-friendly version, use crafts foam to make hearty pots for the front step.

SUPPLIES

Small flowerpot; pink crafts paint; paintbrush
Papers in red and pink; scissors; marking pens; chenille stems
Stapler and staples; tape
Fishbowl rocks or packages of colored stones

WHAT TO DO

1 Paint the flowerpot with crafts paint. Let the paint dry. Fold the red and pink papers in half and cut out half hearts with center along fold. Unfold each heart.

2 Write a message on each heart. Form a heart shape with the chenille stems, leaving a long tail.

3 Staple each chenille stem to a paper heart. If needed, put a piece of tape over the hole in the bottom of the pot. Pour the rocks into the pot. Arrange the hearts and chenille stems in the pot.

SHOW YOUR FRIENDS AND FAMILY HOW MUCH YOU LOVE THEM BY MAKING THIS SWEET VALENTINE'S DAY GIFT. BUT BE PREPARED FOR SOME HUGS AND KISSES IN RETURN!

Clay Coasters

BAKE A SET OF SWIRLED COASTERS TO GIVE WITH LOVE.

SUPPLIES

*Polymer clay, such as Sculpey, in pearl
  lavender, red, dusty rose, and translucent*
*Rolling pin; crafts knife; rubber stamps in kiss,
  heart, and swirl motifs*
Gold pigment ink; new pencil with eraser top
Baking sheet
Satin polymer glaze, such as Sculpey
Glue, such as Fast Grab; small cork pads

WHAT TO DO

1 For the kiss coaster, knead pearl lavender clay with hands. Knead translucent clay. Mix together lavender clay and translucent clay in equal proportions. Mix in a small piece of red clay to pearl lavender clay to create red streaks. Roll clay out and square clay edges up with a crafts knife. Moisten kiss stamp with gold ink. Press into center of clay coaster. Moisten top of new pencil eraser in gold ink. Press into coaster several times; reink after each press.

2 For gold heart-stamp coaster, knead red clay with hands. Knead translucent clay. Mix together red clay and translucent clay in equal proportions. Roll clay out and square edges up with a crafts knife. Moisten heart stamp with gold pigment ink. Press into clay coaster in rows right side up and upside down. Reink stamp after each press.

3 For the large red heart coaster, knead lavender clay with hands. Knead translucent clay. Mix together lavender clay and translucent clay in equal proportions. Knead together red clay and dusty rose clay. Knead translucent clay and red-rose mix. Roll clay mix out and cut a heart pattern out using a crafts knife. Cut heart into three sections. Roll lavender clay out and square edges up with a crafts knife. Press heart sections into lavender clay coaster. Moisten the swirl stamp with gold ink. Press into heart sections several times, reinking after each press.

4 For all coasters, bake according to manufacturer's directions on a baking sheet. Apply a thin layer of the glaze to the top of each coaster and bake another 6 to 7 minutes in 275° oven. Glue cork pads to coaster bottoms.

Bright Idea
......
Use foam to make place mats for other holidays, such as egg shapes for Easter and pumpkins for Halloween.

Be Mine Coasters and Place Mats

SUPPLIES

Tracing paper; pencil; scissors; magenta crafts foam (1 large sheet makes
  1 place mat and 1 coaster); checkerboard stencil
Acrylic paints in fuchsia, mulberry, cardinal red, and metallic gold
Rounded paintbrush; thin paintbrush

WHAT TO DO

1 Enlarge and trace the heart pattern, *opposite*; cut out.

2 Lay place mat heart pattern and coaster pattern on one piece of foam. Trace with a pencil. Cut shapes out using scissors. Repeat process for each place setting.

3 Lay checkerboard stencil midway down heart and trace one row of squares with a pencil. Repeat this for each heart. Begin painting bottom of heart with fuchsia in small sweeping strokes. Paint sweeping strokes of mulberry and cardinal red. Finish with small sweeping dabs of metallic gold. Paint the checkerboard metallic gold and mulberry. Paint the top of heart in mulberry with swirling strokes of fuchsia and cardinal red. Outline each heart with a thin line of mulberry. Let paint dry.

CELEBRATE VALENTINE'S DAY WITH LIGHTHEARTED PLACE MATS AND COASTERS CUT FROM FOAM.

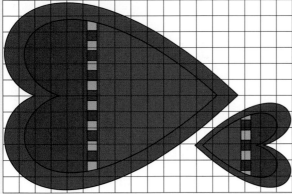

**Be Mine Coaster and
Place Mat Patterns**

1 Square =
1 Inch

**Talk With
Your Kids**
Ask them
who they
want to
remember
on
Valentine's
Day.

Marbled Paper Valentine Cards

SUPPLIES

Newspapers; old rectangular pan
Stained glass color spray, such as Krylon, in purple, red, and green
Red frosted glass finish spray, such as Krylon; metallic gold spray paint
Interior-exterior spray paint in blue gloss and watermelon; waxed paper
Metallic gold leafing pen; tracing paper; pencil; scissors; ruler
Cardboard (optional); card stock in ivory, yellow, burgundy, red, black, and
    textured metallic gold; adhesive foam mounts, such as Mini Pop Dots
Double-sided tape; disposable gloves (optional)

SPREAD LOVING THOUGHTS WITH THESE LOVELY HANDMADE GREETINGS.

WHAT TO DO

1 Cover work surface with newspapers. Fill pan halfway full with water. Spray water with desired paint. (*Note:* All colors of paints and card stocks were used to make marbled papers for the multiple heart card. For the red hearts card, use red card stock, red stained glass color spray, red frosted glass finish spray, metallic gold spray paint, and watermelon interior-exterior spray paint.)

2 Lay card stock on top of water surface and gently submerge it. Lift card stock out of water and allow to dry on a piece of waxed paper. If desired, dip card stock again to increase effects. Try experimenting with different color combinations of paint and card stock. Each type of spray paint (stained glass color, frosted glass finish, and interior-exterior) has a different effect on paper. Skim leftover paint from water using a piece of cardboard or extra paper. Change the water periodically.

3 To make a pattern, trace the heart *below right,* or draw a heart the desired size and cut it out. For the multiple hearts card, measure and cut a 10×7-inch card from burgundy card stock. Fold card in half. Using pattern, cut out nine hearts from several colored marbled papers. Trim the edges of the hearts with the gold leafing pen. Cut two strips of marbled paper ¼×5 inches. Trim one edge of each strip with gold leafing pen.

4 Adhere the strips to the top and bottom edges of the front of the card using double-sided tape. Apply the hearts to the front of the card using foam mounts. Stack foam mounts two and three high underneath some of the hearts for a multilevel dimensional look.

5 For the red heart card, measure and cut a 10×7½-inch card from black card stock. Fold card in half. Measure and cut a rectangular piece of red marbled paper approximately 4¼×6¾ inches. Outline the edges of the red marbled paper with the gold leafing pen. Center and tape paper to the front of the card.

6 Cut out a small heart from additional red marbled paper. Outline the edges of the heart with the gold leafing pen. Cut out medium heart from gold textured paper, enlarging pattern provided. Cut large heart from red card stock. Adhere hearts to each other and to the front of the card with foam mounts for extra dimension.

Valentine Card Heart Pattern

THE FUN GOES ON AFTER THE DIPPING AND DYEING IS DONE. MAKE PATTERNS ON YOUR EASTER EGGS USING COLORFUL STICKERS!

Bright Idea
......
Use Easter stickers from scrapbook stores to decorate eggs.

Polka-Dot Eggs

SUPPLIES

Hard-boiled or blown-out white or brown eggs
Egg-dyeing kit or food coloring
Small round colored stickers and/or colored reinforcements
  (available at office supply stores)

WHAT TO DO

1 Dye the white eggs using an egg-dyeing kit, or mix 1 tablespoon of food coloring with 1 cup of water.

2 Drop eggs carefully into colored water and let soak for about 10 minutes. Take the eggs out of the water. Let dry.

3 Decide how you want to put the stickers on the eggs. Make polka dots, faces, flowers, or whatever you like on the colored or brown eggs.

Easter Egg Mats

SUPPLIES
Pencil; tracing paper; crafts foam; scissors; thick white crafts glue

WHAT TO DO
1 Trace egg shapes, *pages 198–199;* cut them out. Draw around the pattern on the background color of crafts foam. Cut out the shape.

2 Using the patterns for ideas, cut shapes from foam and glue to one side of the egg. Let the glue dry.

continued on page 198

USE COLORFUL FOAM TO MAKE VIVID EGG COASTERS.

Talk With Your Kids
Talk about what flavors of jelly beans the kids like and have a contest for the strangest combo.

197

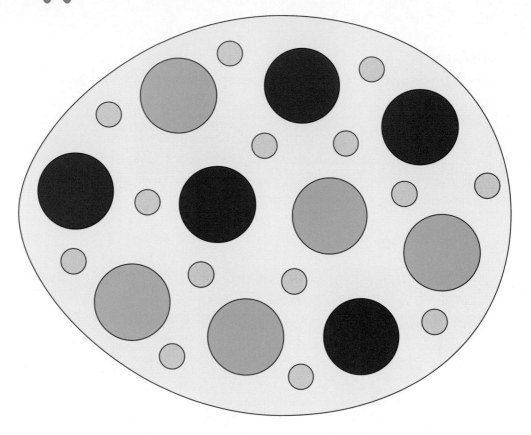

Bright Idea
......
Enlarge the patterns and make a set of place mats.

Easter Egg Mats Patterns

198

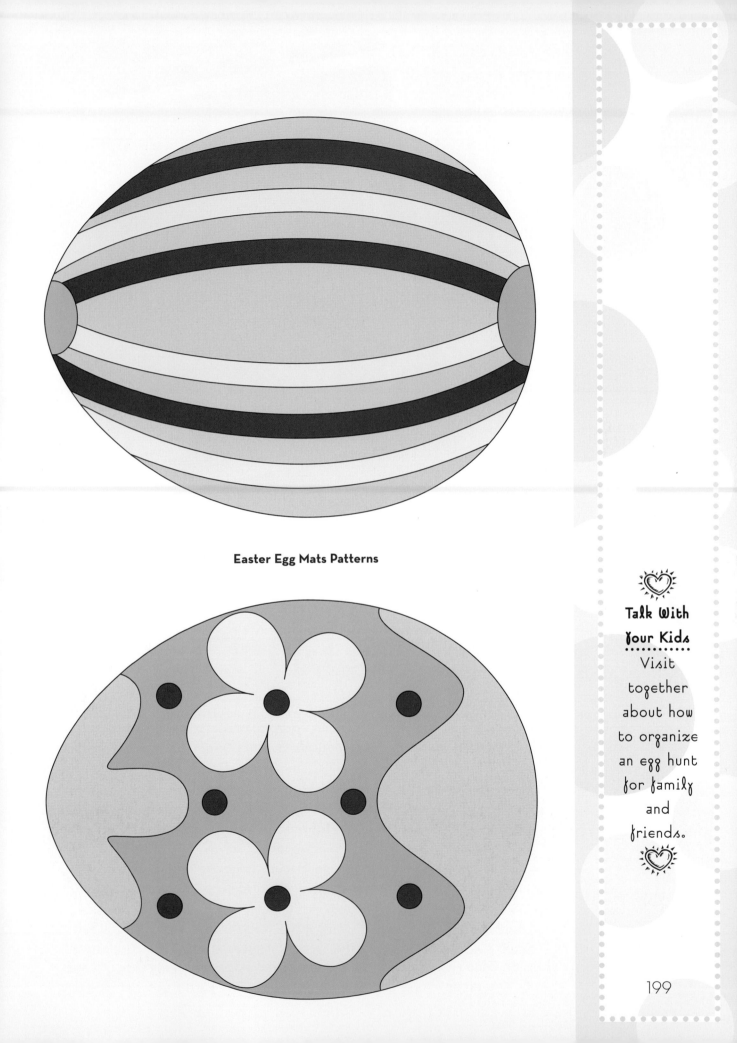

Easter Egg Mats Patterns

Talk With Your Kids

Visit together about how to organize an egg hunt for family and friends.

Bright Idea
......
Sew two larger felt eggs and insert a foam form to make an "egg-sotic" throw pillow.

A SAMPLING OF STITCHES GIVES INTRICATE DETAIL TO THIS FELT DESIGN.

Fun with Felt

SUPPLIES
Felt in bright pink, yellow, green, and purple; scissors; ruler; embroidery floss; needle; white card stock; purple rickrack; plain note card; envelope

WHAT TO DO

1 Cut an egg shape from bright pink felt, making it approximately 1 inch smaller than the card. Cut out four nickel-size circles from yellow felt.

2 Arrange circles on egg; tack in place using French knots. Trim off circles extending beyond the egg edge. Secure edges with blanket stitches.

3 Using the photo, *above*, as a guide, decorate the remainder of the felt egg using a variety of stitches.

4 Glue the egg to green felt; trim a narrow border. Glue to purple felt and cut a rectangular border. Glue to white card stock; cut a narrow border. Glue rickrack on the top and bottom edges of wrong side of card stock and on envelope flap. Glue the paper to the card front. Let glue dry.

Spring-Fresh Set

SUPPLIES

Raised-design scrapbook frames; fine sandpaper; rag; metal primer
Acrylic paints in lilac, pink, turquoise, and green; pigment ink, such as
 StazOn, in lavender, green, blue-green, and duo red-blue
Small fine paintbrush; loop yarn
Crafts glue; lavender scrapbook paper; black calligraphy marking pen
Scissors; double-sided tape; brushed metallic gold card stock

WHAT TO DO

1 Gently sand the frames; wipe clean. Brush on a coat of metal primer; let dry. Paint one thin coat of acrylic paint (one color at a time) on raised areas of frame. Let dry to a tacky stage. Dip dry brush in coordinating pigment powder and brush on tacky areas. Blow and brush away any excess powder. Repeat with each color of paint and powder; let dry.

2 Cover the frame front with two coats of varnish. Glue a piece of yarn to the top of each frame. Let dry.

3 Write guests' names on lavender paper; cut out to fit the frames. Use double-sided tape to adhere each to a frame back. Using pattern, *below*, cut and fold gold card stock stands. Tape stand ends together; tape stands to the back of frames.

Talk With Your Kids
Read the Easter story and discuss why baby animals are such a big part of this holiday.

FRESH COLORS AND FRILLY FIBERS PRETTY UP A TABLETOP.

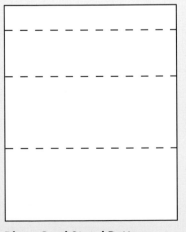

Place Card Stand Pattern

Pretty Pinwheels

SUPPLIES

12-inch-long pieces of ¼-inch-square wood dowels
Acrylic paints in desired colors
Paintbrushes; quilting pins; newspapers; scrapbook papers
Spray adhesive; pencil; ruler; scissors; decorative-edge scissors (optional)
Large round beads; mechanical pencil replacement erasers
Fabric flower stickers (available in scrapbook stores)

WHAT TO DO

1 Paint the dowel and let it dry. Choose a contrasting color of paint for details. Paint stripes, checks, dots, or other simple designs on the dowel. Let dry.

2 Push a pin through the dowel ½ inch from one end. Remove the pin.

3 Cover work surface with newspapers. Choose two contrasting scrapbook papers. Turn one sheet facedown on the newspapers and spray the back with adhesive. Align the contrasting paper, faceup, on the adhesive and press.

Choose colorful scrapbook papers and paints to make summery celebration pinwheels.

4 For each pinwheel, use a ruler to mark a 6- to 7-inch square. (*Note:* If using 12-inch-square scrapbook papers, cut in half each way to make four pinwheels from each adhered sheet.) Draw an X from corner to corner.

5 Cut out the square using straight-edge or decorative-edge scissors. Use straight scissors to cut along the lines of the X, stopping 1 inch from the center of the paper for each of the four cuts.

6 Use a pin to carefully poke a hole in every other pinwheel blade approximately ½ inch from the tip. Working clockwise, bend the points to the center of the pinwheel while sliding a pin through all the holes.

7 Slide a bead on the pin, thread it through the dowel hole, and secure it with an eraser. Press a sticker on the head of the pin.

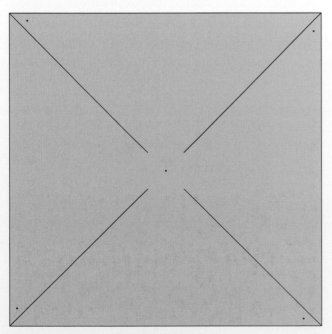

Pinwheel Diagram

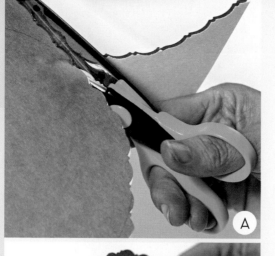
A

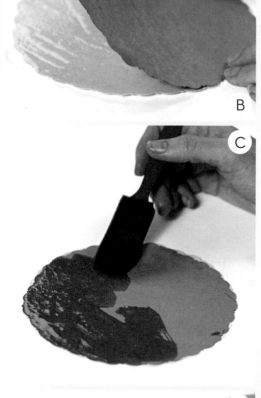
B

C

KIDS LOVE TO MAKE AND FILL THESE MINI PAPER BASKETS! ONCE THEY LEARN HOW TO STIFFEN PAPER WITH LIQUID STARCH, THEY CAN USE THEIR BIG IMAGINATIONS TO MAKE ALL SORTS OF WONDERFUL TREASURES.

SUPPLIES

Large paper plate; pencil
Large sheets of construction paper
Wrapping paper (optional)
Decorative-edge scissors
Foam paintbrush; liquid starch
Jar or glass; rubber bands
Hole punch; chenille stems

WHAT TO DO

1 Trace around a paper plate on construction paper and wrapping paper if desired. Use decorative-edge scissors to cut out two circles as shown in Photo A, *left*.

2 Brush one circle generously with liquid starch. Place the remaining circle on the wet circle to stick them together as shown in Photo B. Brush on another coat of liquid starch as shown in Photo C.

3 Center the layered circles on a jar or glass and form the circles to the curve. Hold the papers in place with a rubber band

D

Talk With Your Kids

Talk about the importance of doing nice things for others and make May baskets for residents of a local nursing home.

as shown in Photo D. Fluff out the edges of the paper circles. Let set for several hours until dry.

4 Remove the papers from the jar. Punch holes on opposite sides and thread a chenille stem through the holes, shaping it into a handle. Twist the chenille stem ends to secure.

Ruffled May Baskets

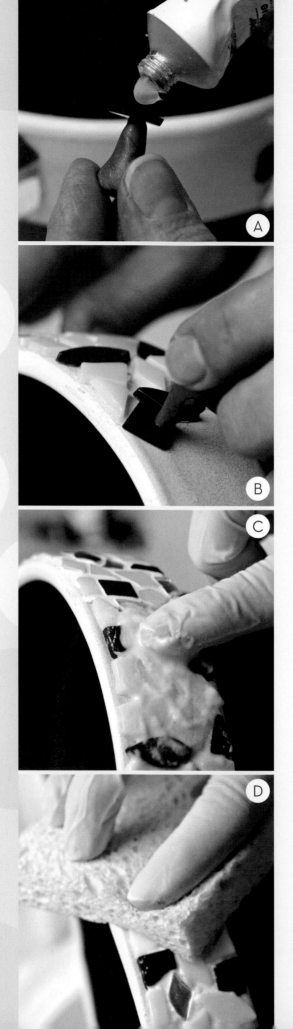

A

B

C

D

COAT FLOWERPOTS WITH EYE-CATCHING ACRYLIC PIECES IN STAR-SPANGLED RED, WHITE, AND BLUE.

SUPPLIES

6-inch terra-cotta flowerpots
Newspapers; white interior-exterior primer spray; blue gloss interior-exterior spray paint
2 packages of clear/ivory/silver acrylic pieces, such as Clearly Mosaics Designer Color Multis
Pencil; clear silicone sealer adhesive
Small piece of clay; sponge
1 package each of blue marbleized and red acrylic pieces, such as Clearly Mosaics
Ivory grout, such as Clearly Mosaics
Plastic bowl; masking tape

WHAT TO DO

1 For the multicolor-rim pot, spread out newspapers and spray pot inside and out with white primer. Let dry. Cover rim of pot with masking tape. Spray pot with two coats of blue gloss spray paint on the inside and on the bottom outside of pot, allowing time to dry between coats.

2 Adhere mosaic pieces to pot rim randomly with silicone sealer, using clay to pick up the individual pieces as shown in Photos A and B. Let dry 24 hours before grouting.

3 For the stars and stripes mosaic pot, spread out newspapers and spray terra-cotta pot inside and out with white primer. Let dry. Spray two coats of blue paint inside the pots, allowing time to dry between coats.

4 Separate silver acrylic pieces to form star patterns. Plan the pot rim star locations and spacing.

Mosaic 4th of July Celebration Pots

Mark spacing lightly with pencil. Adhere silver acrylic star pieces to pot rim with silicone sealer, using clay to pick up the individual pieces as shown in Photos A and B.

5 Apply blue acrylic pieces to rim between the stars. Create vertical red stripes with acrylic pieces centered between stars. Apply the silver stripes. Let silicone dry 24 hours before grouting.

6 Follow manufacturer's directions to grout between the acrylic pieces as shown in Photos C and D. Let grout dry 24 hours before using.

CHAPTER 6

Accents for Outdoors

Sprinkle your talents and creativity all around the yard with oodles of projects to entertain the whole clan.

BRING THE OUTDOORS IN WITH INVENTIVE PROJECTS TO ENLIVEN YOUR HOME, SUCH AS THE BIRD, *OPPOSITE*, AND HIS HOUSE, *LEFT*. THE LEAF NECKLACE IS SCULPTED FROM OVEN-BAKE CLAY IN LOVELY FALL COLORS.

Autumn Time

Found-Treasures Birdhouse

SUPPLIES

Screw eye; assembled pine birdhouse (available in crafts stores)
8-inch-diameter grapevine wreath; orange acrylic paint; paintbrush
Thick white crafts glue; dried Texas grass (or thin twigs); 3-inch-long
 preserved leaves; 2 acorns; 1 large and 3 small pinecones; twine

WHAT TO DO

1 Attach a screw eye to the top of the birdhouse for hanging. Paint the house orange. Let the paint dry.

2 Glue grass to the side of the house. Overlap and glue leaves on the roof, arranging in rows. Start at the bottom and work to the top. Glue acorns and small pinecones at the top. Wrap the bottom with grapevine.

3 Remove a few scales from a large pinecone. Glue the pieces around the birdhouse opening. Thread twine through the screw eye to hang.

Charmed Necklace

WHAT TO DO

1 For leaves, mix together yellow, green, and orange clay. Using dowel, roll clay until it is 1/4 inch thick. Cut out seven leaves. Use a toothpick to draw veins. For each leaf, press a thick green clay stem; insert one eyelet in each side. Poke toothpick through eyelets to open centers.

2 For beads, roll purple and pieces of other colors into pea-size balls. Push a toothpick through each ball; place an eyelet over each end of toothpick; press eyelets toward center. Use toothpick to open center of bead. Bake clay shapes according to package directions. Let cool.

3 String beads as shown in photo, *right*. Knot the ends.

SUPPLIES

Polymer clay, such as Sculpey, in yellow, green, orange, and purple
Wood dowel; ruler
Miniature leaf-shape cookie cutters
1/8-inch-diameter eyelets
Toothpicks; baking sheet
Elastic beading thread

Feathered Friend

SUPPLIES

Newspapers; small real or artificial fall leaves
Paintbrush; small sponge; acrylic paints in green, orange, yellow, purple, and red
Plastic foam shapes, such as Styrofoam: one 2 7/8×3 3/16-inch egg and one 2-inch-diameter ball
2 small forked branches; 2 acorn caps; 2 toothpicks
Yellow polymer clay, such as Sculpey; plastic knife
Scissors; foam glue, such as Hold the Foam

WHAT TO DO

1 Cover work surface with newspapers. Lay leaves on top. Paint leaves with polka dots, stripes, or sponge prints.

continued on page 212

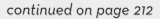

Talk With Your Kids

Go on a family nature walk. Talk about the things you see—birds, plants, flowers—and which are your favorites.

Autumn Time continued

2 Paint the foam egg purple, the ball green, and the branches yellow. Let dry. Paint red stripes on the branches. Paint acorn caps red on outsides, yellow on insides; let dry. Make a purple dot in the center of each cap; let dry. Highlight with red dots.

3 Insert one toothpick into foam ball until ¼ inch of the toothpick shows. Shape clay into a cone beak; push onto toothpick. Push other toothpick halfway into wide end of egg. Push foam ball onto the toothpick for head.

4 Use a knife to make slits in body for leaf feathers. Trim the bottom of each leaf into a V. Dab glue on Vs; push into slits. Dab tops of legs with glue; push into body. Dab tips of acorn caps with glue; push into head for eyes.

Wild-Bird Treat

SUPPLIES

Tracing paper; pencil; scissors; masking tape
Plastic mesh needlepoint canvas; twine; waxed paper; table knife
Peanut butter; black oil sunflower seeds; millet

WHAT TO DO

1 Trace the leaf pattern, *page 214,* onto tracing paper. Cut out the pattern. Tape the pattern to plastic canvas. Cut out the shape. Thread twine at the top of the leaf for hanging.

2 Place leaf on waxed paper; spread with peanut butter. Place sunflower seeds for veins. Sprinkle millet over the leaf and pat into place. Shake off excess. Gently turn over the shape. Repeat for the other side. Hang the leaf in a tree.

Glorious Window Clings

SUPPLIES

Waxed paper; ruler; newspapers; crayon sharpener; crayons in leaf colors
Iron; real autumn leaves for patterns; stylus or dry ballpoint pen; scissors
Foam brush; decoupage medium, such as Mod Podge

Bright Ideas
Use acrylic paint to make designs on large dried leaves and scatter them on the kitchen table around a pumpkin.

WHAT TO DO

1 Tear off a 24-inch length of waxed paper; fold it in half so the short ends match. Open waxed paper and lay it over a newspaper-covered work surface. Sharpen crayons onto one half of the waxed paper. Refold waxed paper with crayon shavings inside.

2 To melt shavings, use a dry iron and set the temperature to medium. Cover waxed paper with newspaper. Iron over the newspaper until the shavings melt. (Melted crayon shavings turn into a hot liquid.) Move the iron in circles to blend the melted shavings. Let cool.

3 Place leaves on waxed paper. Trace around leaves with a stylus. Cut out shapes. Use stylus to draw veins.

4 Using a foam brush, paint a light coat of decoupage medium on one side of each leaf; position it on a window. To remove leaves, just peel them off.

Windy-Day Blanket

SUPPLIES

Tracing paper; pencil; scissors; 6×10-inch rectangles of felt: 4 each of orange, lime green, gold, and lavender; 52½×70½-inch red fleece blanket
Iron (optional); water-soluble marking pen; needle
Embroidery floss in assorted colors; waxed paper
Fabric glue; disposable plate; paintbrush

WHAT TO DO

1 Trace the leaf pattern, *page 215,* onto tracing paper. Cut out the shape.

2 Prewash the felt and blanket to avoid shrinkage. Press the felt with an iron if needed. With the marking pen, draw around the leaf pattern on each felt rectangle. Draw and cut out 16 leaves.

3 Cut a length of floss for sewing. Separate length in half so you have two strands of three plies each. Thread one strand into the needle; knot the end.

4 Using a running stitch, sew down middle of leaf to form the main vein. Sew the remaining veins, referring to pattern on *page 215.* Repeat for all leaves. Lay blanket flat; place leaves around the edge.

5 Place one leaf right side down on waxed paper. Squeeze glue onto the plate. Dip paintbrush into glue; brush glue from one leaf center to outside edges. Cover entire leaf with glue. Pick up leaf at bottom of stem and at tip of leaf. Gently place leaf right side up on the blanket; pat in place. Repeat for all of the leaves. Let glue dry for 24 hours.

continued on page 214

Talk With Your Kids
Make sure your kids know to ask for permission before using an iron.

Bright Idea
Use enlarged leaf patterns to cut shapes from decorative papers to use as place mats.

Wild-Bird Treat Pattern

**Windy-Day Blanket
Pattern**

Talk With Your Kids

Take a walk with your kids and try to identify trees from their leaf shapes.

Nested Seeds

Bright Idea

Use small birdbath stands to hold nest feeders.

SUPPLIES

Coconut-fiber plant liner; scissors
Green grapevine; clippers for vine
Gloves; thin wire; artificial grapes (optional)
Artificial eggs (optional)
Acrylic paints in turquoise, dark blue, and light blue (optional)
Paintbrush; spray satin varnish (optional)
Birdseed

WHAT TO DO

1 Use the coconut-fiber liner as it is or trim it if you want a shallower nest. To trim, cut off the edge with a pair of sharp scissors.

2 Trim vines while they are green for the easiest shaping; they are more pliable when they are green. Wear gloves if you like and strip off all the extra leaves. Using several long strands of vine, wind a loop large enough to fit around the top of the liner. Continue to wind the vine in and out until a nest shape is formed. Tuck ends in tightly. The vine turns brown as it dries.

BIRDS FEEL RIGHT AT HOME SNITCHING SEEDS FROM
THESE JUMBO NESTS.

3 Set the liner inside the woven grapevine and use thin wire to attach
the top of the liner onto the grapevine. Weave the wire into the liner
and onto the vine back and forth around the nest. Wind in small sprigs of
artificial grapes if you wish.

4 Paint artificial eggs with turquoise paint. Let dry. Splatter the eggs
with dark blue and light blue paint. Let dry. Spray the eggs with satin
varnish. Let dry. Place eggs in nest and fill with seed.

For
another
bird treat,
use cookie
cutters to
trim
shapes
from
toast.
Coat with
peanut
butter; use
string to
hang them
from a
tree.

Glistening Ice Rings

SUPPLIES

Gelatin ring molds or mini
* foil pie pans*
Plastic disposable cups
Water; cranberries
Sticks; birdseed; string

WHAT TO DO

1 Use a ring mold or place a plastic cup in the center of the pie tin. If using a cup, put some water in it to prevent it from floating in the pie tin. Fill the mold or the pie tin halfway with water as shown in the photo, *opposite*.

2 Arrange the cranberries, sticks, and birdseed in the water. Let the ring freeze until solid.

3 To remove the ring from the mold, run cold water over the back of the ring. Remove the cup. Tie or loop string around the ring and hang in a tree or bush.

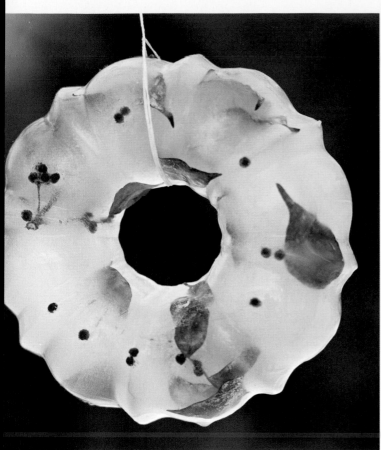

TREAT YOUR
BACKYARD
BIRDS WITH
THESE
BOUNTIFUL ICE
RINGS FILLED
WITH TASTY
DELIGHTS.

Cool Kites

Bright Idea
∙∙∙∙∙∙
To store a kite in the off-season, let your child hang it from the bedroom ceiling.

CHILDREN GLOW WITH PRIDE WHILE WATCHING THEIR ARTWORK SOAR IN THE CLOUDS.

SUPPLIES FOR THE BIRD KITE
18×24-inch piece of lightweight paper; pencil; ruler
Scissors; crayons; watercolor paints
Clear packing tape
Five ¹/₁₆-inch dowels: one 24 inches, one 18 inches,
*   one 10 inches, and two 4 inches in length*
Three 2×48-inch strips of colored cellophane
Nail or needle; 3 feet of string

SUPPLIES FOR THE JAPANESE FIGHTING KITE

18×24-inch piece of lightweight paper; white glue; paintbrush
Colored tissue paper; clear packing tape
Two ¹⁄₁₆-inch dowels: one 24 inches and one 18 inches in length
Nail or needle; 3 feet of string

WHAT TO DO

1 To make either kite, fold paper in half according to the kite pattern, *below*. With a pencil and ruler, mark kite outline on paper following dimensions on pattern. Cut along markings, through both layers of paper.

2 Unfold and create the desired design. For the Japanese Fighting Kite, use a paintbrush to apply glue to a small portion of the kite. Press torn pieces of tissue paper into the glue. Continue this process until entire kite is covered with tissue paper.

3 Turn the kite over; use clear packing tape to affix the dowels to the kite (see diagram). Work on one dowel at a time, placing tape where indicated. (For the Japanese Fighting Kite, two people should work together.) Finish by taping tail pieces at the bottom of the kite. Tails are constructed from the following materials:

Bird Kite: three 2×48-inch strips of colored cellophane

Japanese Fighting Kite: six 1×12-inch strips of tissue paper folded in half

4 Use a nail or needle to poke four holes through the kite where indicated. Turn the kite right side up. Create bow line (see diagram, *below right*) as follows: Drop one end of a 3-foot string through Hole A; bring it back up through Hole B. Tie. Repeat through Holes C and D. Attach kite string to the center of bow line.

Talk With Your Kids

Talk about what it would be like if you could fly.

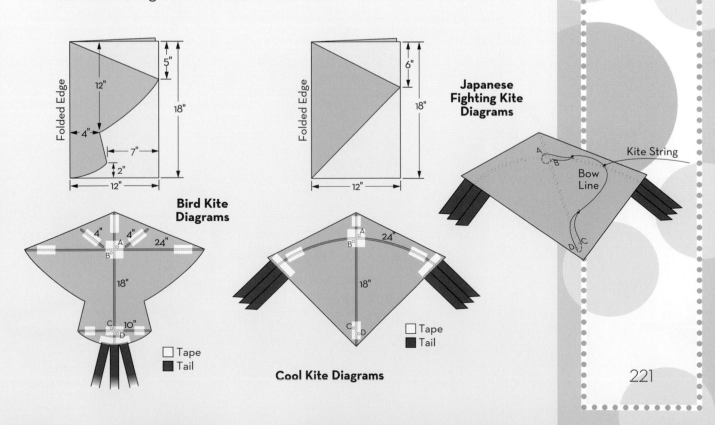

Bird Kite Diagrams

Japanese Fighting Kite Diagrams

Cool Kite Diagrams

□ Tape
■ Tail

Busy Bugs

SUPPLIES

Pom-poms in red, black, yellow, and maroon; thick white crafts glue
Chenille stems in desired colors; small wiggly eyes; quilting thread
Needle; silver thread; ruler; 3 gold rhinestones

WHAT TO DO

1 To make a dragonfly, glue five small red pom-poms together. Using the photo, *below*, as a guide, shape a set of wings from chenille stems. Use one chenille stem for each wing and twist the ends together in the center. Glue the wings to the underside of dragonfly body. Glue two wiggly eyes to the head. Thread a piece of quilting thread through the head to form the antennae. If you like, tie silver thread around each body section.

2 To make the spider, cut red chenille stems into four 3½-inch pieces. Bend each chenille stem piece in half. Sandwich two sets of legs between two black pom-poms. Glue in place. Do this again for a second set of legs. Glue the two sections together. Glue two eyes to the head and three gold rhinestones to the back. Bend the legs into M shapes.

3 To make the caterpillar, cut green chenille stems into four 3½-inch pieces. Bend each chenille stem piece in half. Form the body with five pom-poms and glue a chenille stem between each pair of pom-poms. Bend the ends of each chenille stem to form feet. Glue eyes on the head and thread a piece of quilting thread through head to form antennae.

Bright Idea

Use Busy Bugs as birthday party favors.

No one tries to shoo these fuzzy flies and friends from creeping along your hand or buzzing in your ear!

222

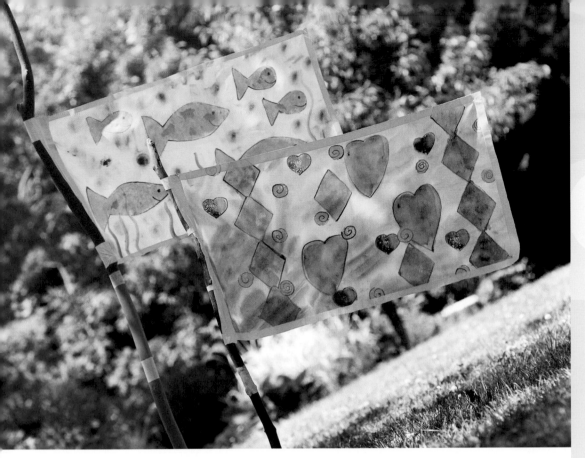

High-Flyin' Flags

PAINT A FLAG TO FLY PROUDLY IN YOUR YARD.

SUPPLIES

Rectangle of nylon fabric (available at fabric stores); water; acrylic paints
Disposable plates; wide paintbrushes; tracing paper; pencil; scissors
Sponges; colored paint markers; stick; colored duct tape

WHAT TO DO

1 Decide on the flag design using the photo, *above*, for ideas. Lay the fabric on a work surface. Spray the fabric with water until it is wet.

2 Put a little of each paint color on a different plate, mixing with water until the paints are runny. Paint the background colors using a wide paintbrush. Blend the colors together some if desired. Let dry.

3 Trace the desired shapes for sponges from *pages 224–225* onto tracing paper; cut out. Trace around the patterns on sponges; cut out.

4 Spread the paint color for stamping onto a plate. Soak the sponges in water and squeeze out. Dip sponge in paint and stamp fabric. Let dry.

5 Outline the shapes with paint markers. Let dry. Paint the stick. Let dry. Press tape around the flag edges. Tape the flag to the stick.

continued on page 224

Talk With Your Kids
Talk about your state flag and what the design symbolizes.

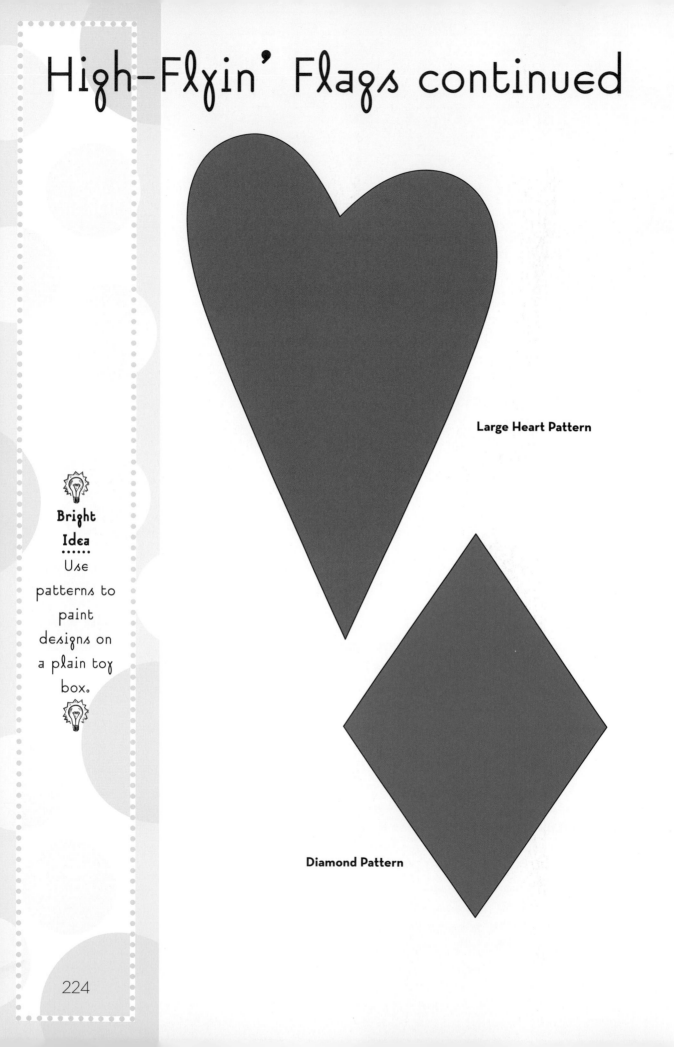

Large Heart Pattern

Diamond Pattern

Bright Idea
......
Use patterns to paint designs on a plain toy box.

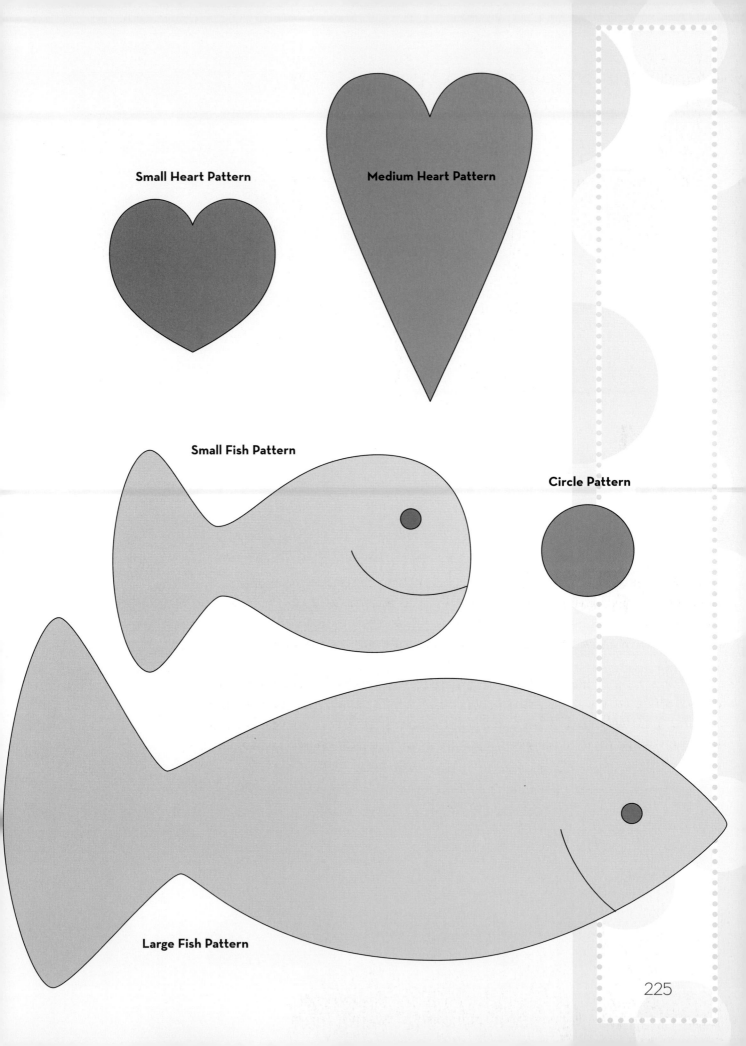

Small Heart Pattern

Medium Heart Pattern

Small Fish Pattern

Circle Pattern

Large Fish Pattern

Marching Band Fun

Happenin' Paper Hat

SUPPLIES

18×20-inch colored paper
Pinking shears; feather

WHAT TO DO

1 Trim the short ends of the paper using pinking shears.

2 Using the diagrams, *below,* fold the paper to make a hat. Tuck a feather into the brim on one side.

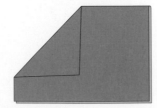

Fold

Hat Folding Diagrams

Make some music with these playful instruments—and wear your paper hat and feather!

Rat-a-Tat Drum

SUPPLIES

Round cardboard
  oatmeal container
Utility knife
Colored paper
Scissors

Glue stick; large balloon; packing tape
Wide rickrack; thick white crafts glue; colored tacks
Colored cording; 1-inch-wide ribbon

WHAT TO DO

1 Using a clean and dry cardboard container, cut off the bottom with a utility knife.

2 Cut a piece of colored paper the same width as the container. Wrap the paper around the container and glue it in place with a glue stick.

3 Cut off the wide, round part of the balloon using scissors. Stretch and pull the balloon over the top of the container. Tape the balloon all the way around the container.

4 Glue a piece of wide rickrack over the tape using crafts glue. Press about four colored tacks around the outer edge of each container end. Press them only partway in, putting glue on each tack point. Starting with one tack, tie colored cording around it and then press the tack in the rest of the way.

5 Wind the cording around tacks to make a zigzag pattern. Knot cording around the last tack.

6 Cut a piece of ribbon for a neck strap to hold drum. Tack each ribbon end onto the drum using a small dab of crafts glue. Let dry.

continued on page 228

Bright Idea

Reserve a box for homemade instruments and get them out on a rainy, inside-play sort of day.

Toot Toot Trumpet

SUPPLIES

Long funnel with a tab and hole at wide end (available in discount stores)
Colored electrical tape; scissors; plastic cording

WHAT TO DO

1 Remove all stickers from the funnel. Wash and dry it. Starting at the narrow end, wrap tape around the funnel until you reach the other end. Fold the tape over the edge and into the inside. Cut off the extra tape. Continue wrapping more tape, using whatever colors you want. Wrap the funnel in tape until it is completely covered.

2 Cut three strands of cording to make a strap. Braid the strap; tie to the tab with the hole. Tape the other end onto the narrow funnel end.

3 Wrap tape around the narrow end to make the end look neat and hold the cording in place. If you wish, wrap tape along the inside edge of the funnel.

Tambourine Time

SUPPLIES

2 foil pie pans
Toothpick
Chenille stems; jingle bells
Hard dried beans, rice, or other filler to place inside pans for noise
Adhesive foil papers (available in scrapbook stores)
Scissors

WHAT TO DO

1. Place foil pie pans' edges together with the insides of pans facing. Poke 8 to 12 holes around the outer edges with a toothpick. Poke holes through both pans.

2. Keeping the holes together, pull a chenille stem through the pair of pans. Loop it through the hole a couple of times to hold it firmly in place. String a jingle bell onto the chenille stem and wind the chenille stem around the edge of pans, twisting the ends of chenille stems together until all of the holes are laced. String bells wherever you wish. When you are about halfway around the pans, place a handful of dried beans, rice, or other filler inside of pans. Continue lacing the edge of the pans to completely trap the filler.

3. Cut triangular shapes from adhesive papers. Stick the papers on the flat part of the pans in a star pattern.

Clink-Clank Bells

SUPPLIES

Small clay flowerpots
Wood dowels to fit in holes of pots
Saw; ruler
Acrylic paints in desired colors
Paintbrush
Thick white crafts glue
Yarn or cording; scissors
Round wood beads ¹/₂ to
  ³/₄ inch in diameter

WHAT TO DO

1. If you wish, choose several sizes of clay pots as different sizes make different sounds. Choose dowels that fit snugly in the holes. Cut an 8-inch-long piece of dowel for each handle.

2. Paint the pots and dowels whatever colors you wish. Let the paint dry.

3. For each pot, place a dab of glue around the hole in the pot. Cut a piece of yarn 10 inches long. Tie a bead in a knot on one end of the yarn. Pull the yarn through the hole and insert a dowel handle. Let glue dry. Trim off extra yarn.

PRETEND YOU PLAY IN A BIG BRASS BAND WITH THIS STRIPED FUNNEL TRUMPET, A FOIL PAN TAMBOURINE, AND FLOWERPOT BELLS!

Talk With Your Kids
Ask your child if they could play any instrument, what would it be?

229

Color-Splashed Watering Can

SUPPLIES

Tracing paper; pencil; scissors
Adhesive crafts foam sheets; watering can

WHAT TO DO

1 To cut foam shapes, use the patterns, *below*, or create your own shapes. To use the patterns, trace and cut them out. Trace around the shapes on foam; cut out.

2 To layer shapes, cut the center shape smaller than the background shape.

3 Peel off the paper backing from the foam shape. Press the shapes onto the watering can. Press the smaller shapes onto the larger shapes.

ENJOY TENDING TO THE GARDEN WITH THIS BRIGHTLY DECORATED WATERING CAN.

Trim Patterns

LOOK AT ROCKS IN A WHOLE NEW WAY! USE YOUR WILDEST IMAGINATION TO MAKE LIZARDS, TURTLES, ALIENS— WHATEVER YOU DREAM UP!

Sluggy Bugs

SUPPLIES

Rocks and pebbles in interesting shapes and sizes
Acrylic paints in bright colors and black; paintbrushes
Black marking pen; thick white crafts glue

WHAT TO DO

1 Gather cool rocks in many sizes. Wash and dry the rocks. Arrange the rocks to look like an animal or other creature that you like.

2 Paint the large background areas of the rocks first. Let the paint dry. Paint polka dots or other designs on the background or paint small pebbles to glue on later.

3 Use a thin paintbrush to paint stripes. Let the paint dry. When painting the eyes, make some happy, sad, and angry. The eyes on the critters, *above,* use two pebbles, one for the pupil and one for the eyeball. First paint the tiny pebbles black. Paint the slightly larger pebbles a light color or two colors if you want to make eyelids (like the purple and yellow eyes, *above*). Let dry. Make details with a black marking pen.

4 Glue the rocks and pebbles together and let the glue dry, or just lay the pieces together to make a creature.

Talk With Your Kids
Dig up a scoop or two of dirt from the yard and discuss what bugs you and the kids discover.

Creativity Fence

Bright Idea
......
Use a brightly painted fence as a child's headboard.

SUPPLIES

Outdoor latex paints in desired bright colors, such as white, green, yellow, pink, lavender, red, and blue
White primed picket fence (available in home centers)
Old clothes and shoes; paintbrushes; disposable plate
Sponges, including a round stamping sponge with handle

WHAT TO DO

1 When blending colors for a fence, choose shades that look bright and pretty when mixed together. On this fence the kids used aqua, lime green, lavender, pink, yellow, and orange.

2 Begin with a clean, dry fence and wear old clothes and shoes. Blend two or three colors together on one piece of wood. Use a different brush for each color. Use a clean paintbrush to blend the colors together. Do this until the fence piece is completely painted. Let it dry.

3 Pour a little bit of white paint onto a disposable plate. Holding the handle, dip the stamping sponge into paint and press onto the fence.

4 Sponge round shapes in circles to make flowers. Let the paint dry.
Sponge yellow circles in the centers of the flowers. Let the paint dry.
Paint green stems and leaves. Let the paint dry.

MIX AND BLEND COLORS TOGETHER TO MAKE VERY PRETTY FENCING. USE PURE COLORS FOR A FENCE THAT IS BRIGHT AND CHEERY.

Talk With Your Kids
·········
Discuss how important it is not to put anything coated with paint in your mouth.

233

Two Green Thumbs-Up

Garden Gate Welcome

SUPPLIES

Quick-setting cement
$11\frac{5}{8}\times9\frac{1}{4}\times2\frac{1}{2}$-inch foil pan
Small pebbles
Drill and a drill bit large enough to accommodate the poly rope
Paintbrush
Acrylic paints in white, orange, yellow, pink, and green
Water-base, nontoxic gloss interior-exterior varnish
Sponge brush; yellow twisted poly rope

WHAT TO DO

1 Mix the cement according to the manufacturer's directions, adding water until it is the consistency of cream. One bag of cement is enough for two decorations. Pour half of the cement mixture into the foil pan.

2 Place the prepared pan on the floor. Press your hands into the cement to make an imprint. Push pebbles into the cement around the edge. Let the cement dry. Remove the dried plaque from the pan.

3 Drill two holes at the top corners of the plaque. Paint the surface white and let dry. Paint handprints and rocks in bright colors and write a name, date, or message.

4 Use the sponge brush to apply several coats of varnish. For the hanging loop, insert a length of rope into the holes and knot the ends.

MAKE A LASTING IMPRESSION WITH CEMENT AND YOUR HANDPRINTS.

Busy Bugs Plant Markers

SUPPLIES

Tracing paper; round pencil; scissors
9¼×12-inch sheets of lightweight copper
Crafts foam in pink, orange, and yellow; sparkling modeling wire mesh
³⁄₁₆-inch hole punch; copper wires in 16- and 24-gauge; wire cutters
Golf tees; permanent black marking pen; ruler; cabochons; crafts glue
2 green pony beads; 2 orange pony beads; 2 green chenille stems

WHAT TO DO

1 Trace the patterns on *page 237* onto tracing paper; cut out.

2 Use the pencil to draw around the patterns onto the copper sheets and the crafts foam. From copper, cut out two grasshopper wings and one pair of ladybug wings. From crafts foam, cut out a pink butterfly, yellow dragonfly wings, a yellow firefly body, and one orange ladybug body.

continued on page 236

Two Green Thumbs-Up continued

Cut small and large firefly wings from the wire mesh. Punch 3/16-inch holes as indicated on the patterns, folding the wings and bodies in half to reach inaccessible areas.

3 Cut a long piece of 16-gauge wire; wrap it around the pencil to make a long coil. Slip the pointed end of a golf tee through the bottom two or three coils and then tighten those coils down around the tee. Make one for each plant marker.

4 Write the name of the plant on the foam or copper using the permanent marking pen.

5 To attach the bugs to the coils, punch two holes near each bug's center. Slip the top coil of the golf-tee assembly through the holes. Pinch the coil to secure.

6 For the butterfly, cut a 6-inch length of 24-gauge copper. Referring to the photo on *page 235*, push the ends through the foam at the tiny circles on the pattern. Twist the wire together close to the foam. Curl the ends to make antennae. Glue cabochons to the wings at the Xs.

7 For the dragonfly, cut a 2×3½-inch piece of copper. Starting at one long edge, roll the copper into a cone, referring to the photo on *page 235*. Trim the ends. Randomly wrap body with thin copper wire, adding green pony-bead eyes and wire antennae at the head. Attach the body to the wing/golf-tee assembly, stitching through the punched holes.

8 For the firefly, cut 4-inch lengths of thin wire for the legs and 2-inch lengths for the antennae. Push each wire halfway through the foam body at the tiny circles. Twist the ends together; trim to the desired length. Place the large mesh wings on the small wings. Attach the wings to the body at the center circles with a length of thin wire. Twist the ends of the wire securely to the top of the coiled golf-tee assembly. Glue cabochon eyes to head at Xs. Curve wings.

9 For the grasshopper, cut a 3×4-inch piece of wire mesh. Referring to the photo on *page 235*, roll the mesh into a 4-inch-long curve about 3/4 inch in diameter. Press the tail end flat. Trim across the tail. Holding the tail horizontally, press the head flat on the vertical. Trim the head in a light curve. Use thin wire to stitch orange pony-bead eyes to the head. Twist the wire ends to secure. Cut a 6-inch length from one green chenille stem. Bend the stem at the elbows and wrists. Starting ½ inch from arms, push a full-length chenille stem halfway through the body. Punch holes in the copper wings. Slip a wing on each chenille stem end. Use a piece of thin wire to secure the wings. Bend the chenille stem at the knees and ankles.

10 For the ladybug, cut 2-inch lengths of thin wire for the legs and antennae. Referring to the photo on *page 235*, push each wire halfway through the foam body at the tiny circles. Twist ends together; trim to desired length. Glue cabochon eyes to the head at the Xs.

continued on page 238

Bright Idea
......
Use decorative plant markers to enhance your indoor greenery.

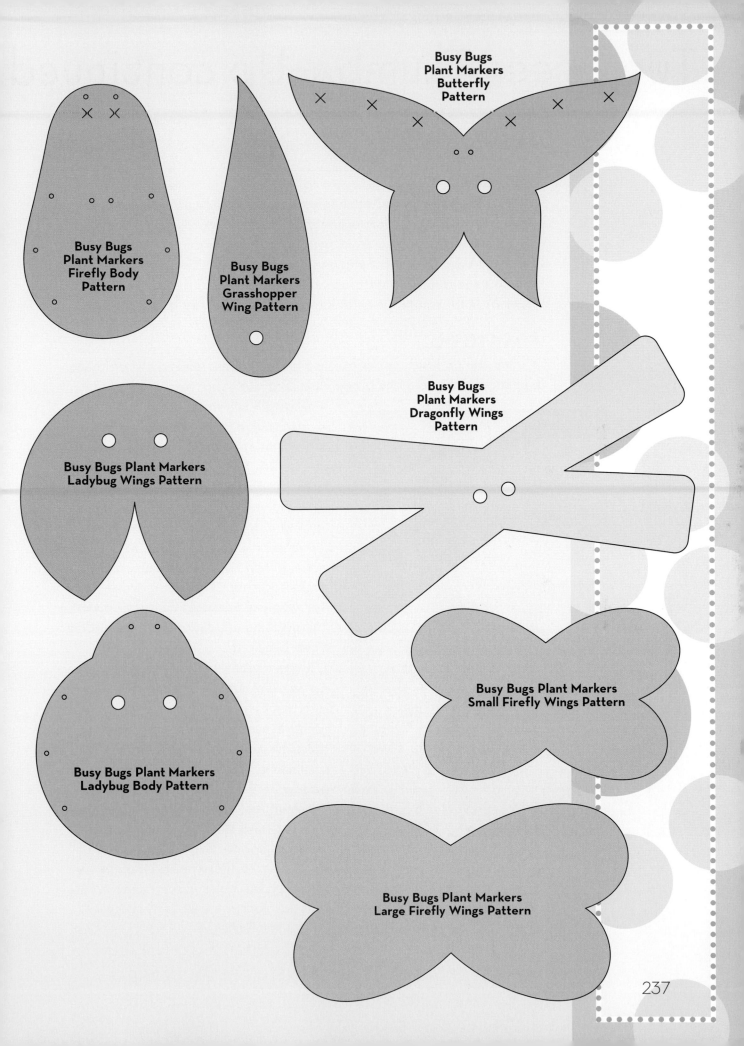

Busy Bugs
Plant Markers
Firefly Body
Pattern

Busy Bugs
Plant Markers
Grasshopper
Wing Pattern

Busy Bugs
Plant Markers
Butterfly
Pattern

Busy Bugs Plant Markers
Ladybug Wings Pattern

Busy Bugs
Plant Markers
Dragonfly Wings
Pattern

Busy Bugs Plant Markers
Small Firefly Wings Pattern

Busy Bugs Plant Markers
Ladybug Body Pattern

Busy Bugs Plant Markers
Large Firefly Wings Pattern

237

Megan's Garden Flag

SUPPLIES

Pencil; tracing paper; self-healing mat; ruler; rotary cutter; scissors
Tablecloth plastic in yellow, orange, red, and green; ³/₁₆-inch hole punch
Fabric glue; teal paint pen; black permanent marking pen or black paint pen
Drill and ³/₈-inch drill bit; 2 sticks (³/₈ inch and ¹/₄ inch in diameter)
Wood glue (optional); paintbrush; orange acrylic paint; sponge brush
Water-base gloss interior-exterior varnish; blue plastic cording

WHAT TO DO

1 Trace the patterns, *opposite*, onto tracing paper. Make a mirror image of the flower along the broken line. Cut out.

2 Using a self-healing mat, ruler, and rotary cutter or scissors, cut a 10×28-inch rectangle from yellow plastic for the flag. With scissors, cut an orange flower, red center, and green leaves.

3 Fold yellow plastic in half crosswise. Mark dots across the top, spacing them ³/₄ inch from the fold and ³/₄ inch apart; punch holes. Glue bottom edges together.

4 Apply glue evenly over the flower pieces and adhere them to the flag front. Let dry.

5 Use the teal paint pen to draw the broken outlines. Write the words with black.

6 Drill a hole in the top of the large stick just big enough to hold the small stick. Check the fit and secure with wood glue if you like.

7 Paint the sticks orange. Let dry. Paint on two to three coats of varnish using the sponge brush.

8 Cut an 18-inch length of plastic cording. Make a knotted loop in one end and thread the other end through the holes in the flag to create a casing. Make another knotted loop at the opposite end. Trim excess cording. Slide loops and casing over the small stick.

PAINTED STICKS AND TABLECLOTH PLASTIC MAKE A BRIGHT MARK AT YOUR SPECIAL SPOT IN THE YARD.

**Megan's Garden Flag
Left Leaf Pattern**

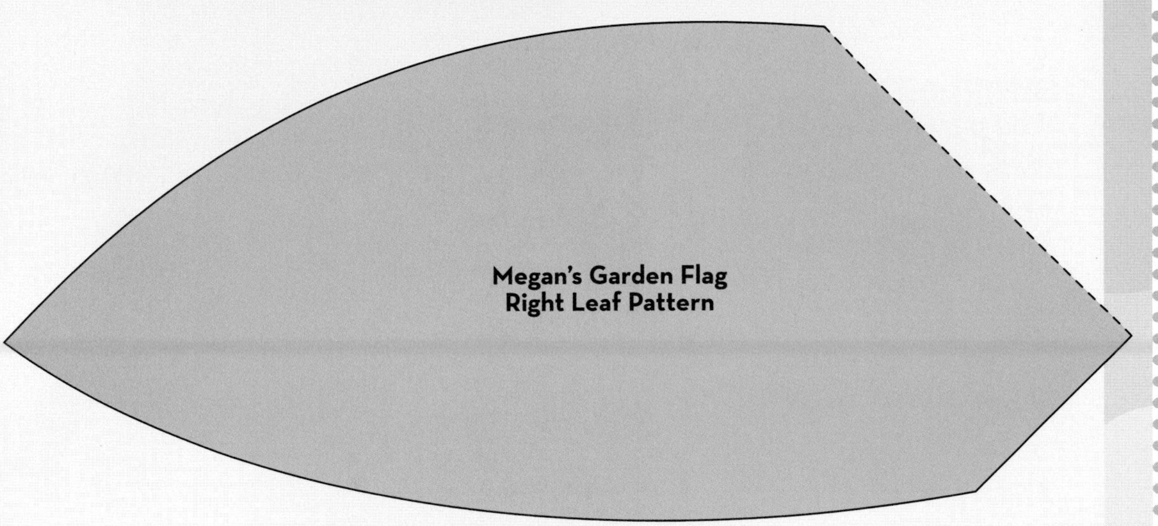

**Megan's Garden Flag
Right Leaf Pattern**

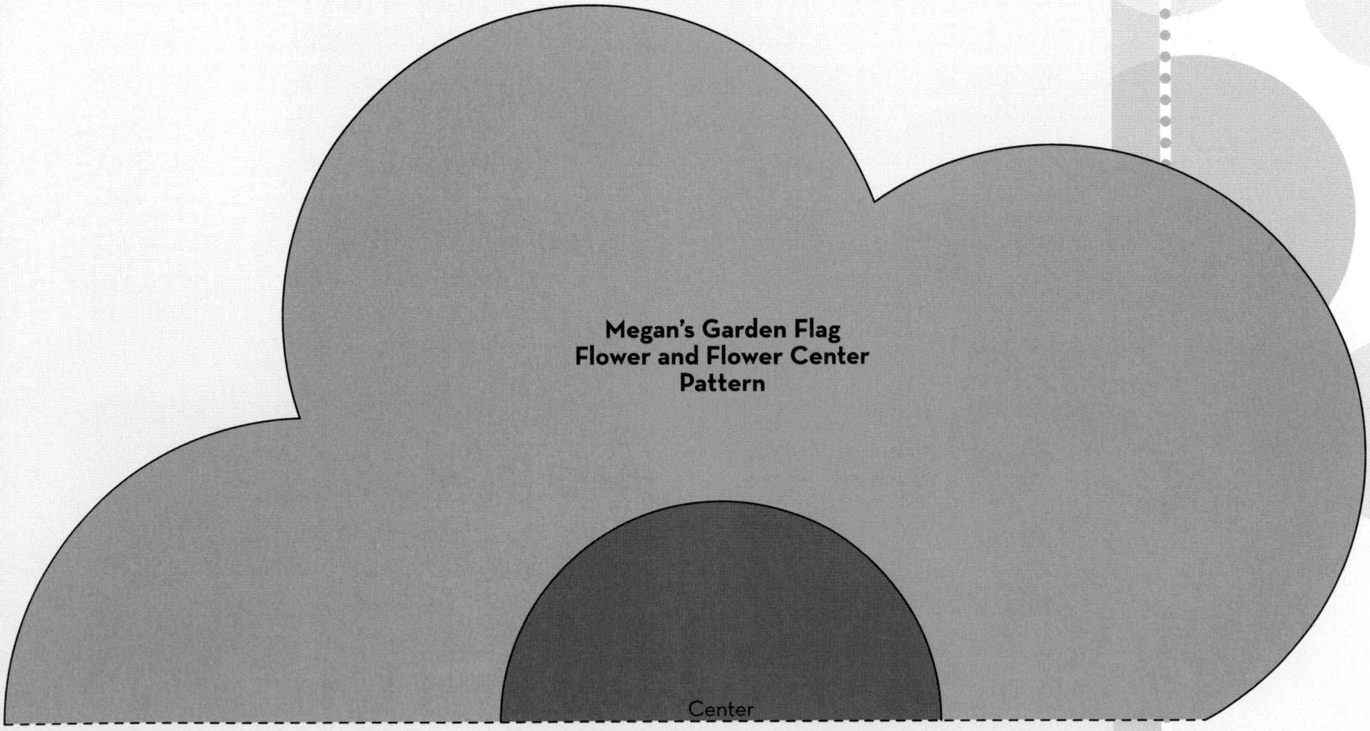

**Megan's Garden Flag
Flower and Flower Center
Pattern**

Center

**Talk With
Your Kids**
Talk about
ways you
can all
contribute
to the
family
garden.

Stick-to-It Easel

THIS STICK FRAME IS SO NEAT, YOU'LL GET REQUESTS TO MAKE ONE FOR ALL YOUR FRIENDS!

Bright Idea
......
Make the entire picture with sticks. Arrange smaller sticks inside each frame.

SUPPLIES
Four 9-inch-long sticks
Thick white crafts glue
Embroidery floss
Drawing or painting glued to cardboard
Eight 6-inch-long sticks to fit around picture
Pliers or wire cutters

WHAT TO DO

1 For easel, make an A with three 9-inch sticks; glue to hold. Let dry. Apply more glue at corners and wrap with floss several times as shown in Photo A. Apply a little bit of glue to the fourth stick and place it against the top two. While holding it in place, wrap floss around all three sticks at the top as shown in Photo B.

2 For frame, use pliers to break off four sticks the same lengths as the cardboard edges. Glue the sticks to the edges. Break four more sticks to fit inside the stick frame. Put glue in the middle of each stick and wrap the sticks with floss; glue to the inside of the frame as shown in Photo C. Let dry.

Nature Frame

SUPPLIES

Frame; decoupage medium; paintbrush; clovers, leaves, ferns, or other fresh flat greenery; 2 mats; picture or drawing; tape

WHAT TO DO

1 Starting with the frame, cover the entire front and sides with decoupage medium. Arrange the greenery on the frame, pressing the pieces in place. Apply two more coats of decoupage medium, letting it dry between coats.

2 Decoupage greenery onto the mats the same way as for the frame. Let dry. Tape a photo or drawing in place behind the mats and insert into the frame.

TAKE A NATURE WALK AND GATHER A HANDFUL OF CLOVER AND INTERESTING-SHAPE LEAVES TO MAKE AN OUT-OF-THIS-WORLD PICTURE FRAME.

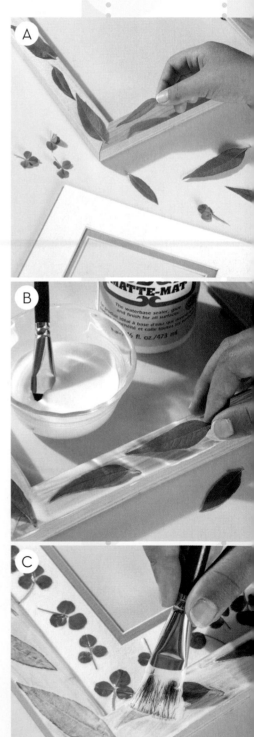

241

Handcrafted Parties

Make it a family affair and work together to make each
party you host a memorable one.

Sleepover Slippers

Bright Idea
Instead of candy favors, treat your sleepover guests to a new pair of cozy slippers!

SUPPLIES

Tracing paper; pencil; scissors; pink velour scrapbook paper
Green crafts foam; needle
Embroidery floss in pink, yellow-orange, and turquoise
2 buttons each of yellow and red; 3 purple buttons
Thick white crafts glue; 5¼×10½-inch piece of black paper
White paper; ruler; glue stick; decorative-edge scissors
Black fine-line marking pen; 6-inch-square purchased envelope

WHAT TO DO

1 Trace the patterns, *opposite*, and cut out the shapes. Trace around slipper and leaf patterns on pink velour paper and green foam. Cut out.

2 To create each flower center, thread the needle with embroidery floss. Sew through the button holes three or four times so they appear to be sewn on each slipper. Knot the floss on the back. Trim the floss ends. One purple button is for the inside of the card.

3 Using crafts glue, adhere the pink soles to the green foam. Trim ⅛ inch beyond pink. Bend the slipper tops to fit and glue the ends to the soles. Let dry.

4 Glue the button flowers and foam leaves to the slipper tops. Set aside.

5 With the short ends aligned, fold the black paper in half. Measure, mark, and cut thirteen 1-inch squares from white paper. Using a glue stick, adhere the pieces checkerboard-style to the front of the black card. Use crafts glue to hold the slippers in place.

6 For the inside of the card, cut a 4½-inch square from white paper. Glue to a piece of pink velour paper. Using decorative-edge scissors, trim the pink paper close to the white paper. Glue to the inside of the card. Write "It's a

Talk With Your Kids
Make sure you're all on the same page when it comes to sleepover rules.

slippers and pj's sleepover!" on the inside of the card. Glue a button flower and two foam leaves to the lower right-hand corner of the white paper. Place each invitation in an envelope.

MADE FROM PLUSH PAPER, BUTTONS, AND FOAM, MINIATURE SLIPPERS MAKE THE PERFECT INVITATION.

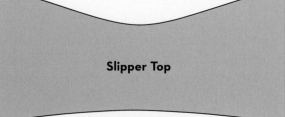

Slipper Sole

Slipper Top

Slipper Leaf

Mylar Favor Bags

SUPPLIES

Tracing paper; pencil; scissors
Hologram Mylar wrapping paper in purple, green, yellow, and red
Hologram Mylar ribbon in fuchsia, purple, blue, and yellow
Double-sided tape; tape

WHAT TO DO

1 For the square bag, enlarge and trace pattern, *opposite*, and cut out. Cut two squares from purple Mylar wrapping paper. Cut one smaller square from green mylar. Center and tape green square on one purple square using double-sided tape. Cut a small circle from yellow Mylar wrapping paper and tape it in the center of the green square. On wrong side of the other purple square, cut and tape yellow ribbon around all edges of square. Tape the two purple squares together on three sides

USE HOLOGRAM PAPER AND RIBBON TO MAKE FLASHY GRAPHIC BAGS TO HOLD PARTY SURPRISES.

using double-sided tape. Fill favor bag and tape the fourth side closed.

2 For the flower bag, enlarge and trace the pattern, *right,* and cut out. Cut two flower shapes from purple Mylar wrapping paper. Cut one smaller flower shape from red Mylar wrapping paper. Center and tape red Mylar wrapping paper to one of the purple flowers using double-sided tape. Cut five small circles from yellow Mylar wrapping paper and tape them onto the red Mylar wrapping paper flower. Tape the two purple flowers together, leaving an opening to fill the favor bag. Tape the remaining area closed after filling the bag.

3 For the triangle bag, enlarge and trace the patterns, *right,* and cut out. Cut two triangles of green Mylar wrapping paper, and the smaller triangles from purple, yellow, and orange paper. Center and tape purple triangle onto one green triangle using double-sided tape. Attach yellow and orange triangles to the purple triangle. Cut four pairs of small slits near the edges of the triangle. Thread hologram ribbons through the slits and tape the ends on the back side using tape. Tape the two triangles of green Mylar wrapping paper together, leaving one side open to fill the favor bag. Tape the remaining side closed after filling the bag.

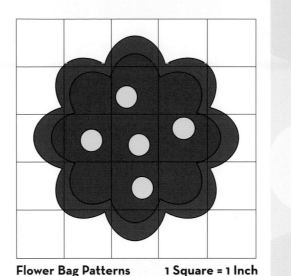

Flower Bag Patterns 1 Square = 1 Inch

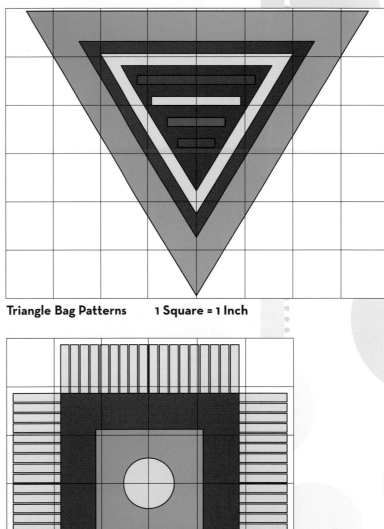

Triangle Bag Patterns 1 Square = 1 Inch

Square Bag Patterns 1 Square = 1 Inch

Talk With Your Kids

Remind the children how important it is to send thank yous.

247

**Bright
Idea**
••••••
Why stop
at the
cases? Let
your kids
personalize
curtains to
match!

Autograph Pillowcases

SUPPLIES

Newspapers; pillowcases in bright pink, lavender, or other desired color
Waxed paper; acrylic paints in bright pink, red, yellow, bright green,
 purple, light pink, white, and orange
Fabric-painting medium; disposable plate
Paintbrushes

248

WHAT TO DO

1 Cover the work surface with newspapers. Line the pillowcase with waxed paper.

2 To use paints, mix small amounts with fabric-painting medium following the product instructions. For the flower pillowcase, ask your friends to paint simple flowers on the pillowcase. Use green to paint the stems and leaves. Paint round swirl flower centers. Paint colorful grass and a sun. Let the paint dry.

3 Using a small paintbrush and purple paint, ask your friends to paint their names several times around a flower center to look like petals. Let the paint dry.

4 Use white paint to highlight the flowers and sun. Let dry. Paint white petals on any remaining flowers. Let the paint dry.

5 For the heart pillowcase, ask your friends to paint bright, open hearts on the pillowcase. Use white paint for their names.

6 Paint colorful circles between the hearts. Let the paint dry.

CELEBRATE FRIENDSHIP WITH A HIP PILLOWCASE THAT SHOWS OFF SIGNATURES OF ALL YOUR BEST BUDDIES!

Lucky Ladybug Invite

SUPPLIES

Tracing paper
Pencil; scissors
Printed scrapbook papers in red, turquoise, and green
Solid papers in black, white, and orange
Hole punch
5×10-inch piece of yellow card stock
Glue stick
Wire; wire cutters
Ruler; straight pin
Large seed beads in black and white
Black fine-line marking pen
5½×7-inch purchased envelope

WHAT TO DO

1 Trace the patterns, *opposite*. Cut out patterns and trace around shapes on the corresponding color of paper. Cut out the pieces.

2 With right sides together, align the ladybug's red wings. Use a paper punch to make symmetrical holes in the wings. Punch out two white eyes. Referring to the photo, *above*, glue the shapes in place on the yellow card.

3 Cut a 6-inch piece of wire. Using a straight pin, poke two holes in the hat just above the ladybug's face. Feed the wire through the holes. Thread 22 black beads and one white bead onto each wire end as shown. Push each wire end back through two or three black beads to secure. Trim the excess wire.

4 Use a black marking pen to write the party information on the inside of the invitation. Make a black dot in the center of each eye.

5 Place each invitation in an envelope.

Bright Idea
• • • • •
Cut fabric pieces to appliqué on a pillow.

250

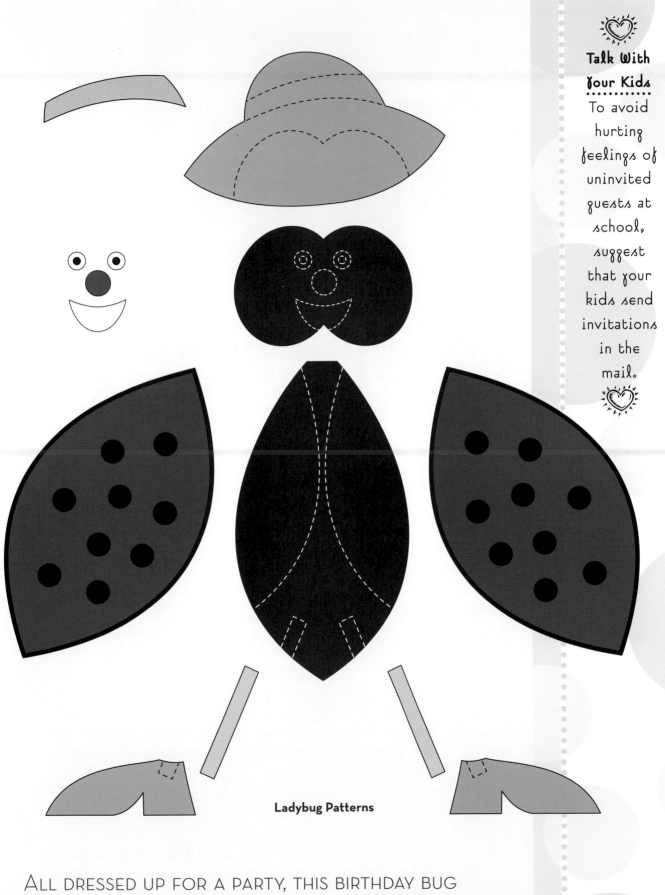

Ladybug Patterns

♥ Talk With
Your Kids
To avoid
hurting
feelings of
uninvited
guests at
school,
suggest
that your
kids send
invitations
in the
mail.
♥

ALL DRESSED UP FOR A PARTY, THIS BIRTHDAY BUG
DELIVERS A WARM WELCOME TO ALL PARTY GUESTS.

KEEP PRESSED PETALS ON HAND YEAR-ROUND TO MAKE DELICATE INVITATIONS.

Pressed Posies Card

SUPPLIES

Heavy card stock; crafts knife; ruler; 1/8-inch-thick white crafts foam
Spray adhesive; pressed flowers; paintbrush; decoupage medium
Solid paper; patterned pastel paper; pencil; envelope

WHAT TO DO

1 Cut heavy card stock to measure 3½×4 inches for the flower background and 10×5½ inches for card. Fold the card piece in half. Trim a piece of foam to 3½×4 inches.

2 Spray one side of foam with adhesive and apply to the background piece of card stock. Arrange flowers on background and brush on decoupage medium as flowers are placed on paper. When all flowers are arranged, brush one final coat of decoupage medium over surface. Reserve some flowers for envelope.

3 Cut a piece of solid paper larger than the inside panel of card. Spray the back side with adhesive. Apply to inside panel, lining up straight edge of paper at the fold. Trim off excess paper with a crafts knife. Repeat the same process for the front card panel using a contrasting paper.

4 On the front panel, measure in ⅝ inch from each edge and draw a light pencil line. Open the card and cut out window using a crafts knife.

5 Close front panel, apply spray adhesive to back of foam, and affix centered through the window onto the inside panel.

6 For the envelope, glue a flower on the flap using decoupage medium.

Bright Idea

Make a pressed posy picture and frame it for the wall.

Pretty Pansy Card

SUPPLIES
Solid paper; scissors; seed packet; thick white crafts glue
Purchased dried flowers; patterned paper; gold writing pen
Hole punch; narrow satin ribbon; purchased envelope

WHAT TO DO
1 Cut solid paper to desired size for card and fold in half. Glue a seed packet on the front of the card.

2 Glue a flower on corner of packet. Cut a piece of patterned paper to fit the inside of the card. Write the desired message.

3 Punch hole in edge of the card. Thread ribbon through the hole. Tie the ribbon into a bow.

4 Choose a coordinating purchased envelope. Glue a dried flower to the flap.

NO MATTER THE SEASON, FLOWERS SEND A SENTIMENTAL MESSAGE. THE SEED PACKET ON THE COVER DOUBLES AS A GIFT FOR PLANTING TIME.

Talk With Your Kids
Talk about the best time of year to plant seeds.

SUPPLIES

- 1 recipe Devil's Food Cupcakes
- 1 recipe Creamy White Frosting
- Small colored gumdrops
- Sugar

DEVIL'S FOOD CUPCAKES

2$^1/_4$	cups all-purpose flour
$^1/_2$	cup unsweetened cocoa powder
1$^1/_2$	teaspoons baking soda
$^1/_4$	teaspoon salt
$^1/_2$	cup shortening
1$^3/_4$	cups sugar
1	teaspoon vanilla
3	eggs
1$^1/_3$	cups cold water

Flower Cupcakes

WHAT TO DO

1 To make cupcakes, grease and lightly flour thirty 2½-inch muffin cups or line with paper baking cups. Preheat oven to 350°. Stir together flour, cocoa powder, baking soda, and salt; set aside.

2 In a large mixing bowl beat shortening with an electric mixer on medium to high speed for 30 seconds. Add sugar and vanilla; beat until well combined. Add eggs one at a time, beating well after each. Add flour mixture and water alternately to shortening mixture, beating on low speed after each addition just until combined.

3 Pour batter into prepared muffin cups, filling each cup halfway. Bake in preheated oven for 15 to 20 minutes or until a wood toothpick inserted in center of a cupcake comes out clean. Cool on a wire rack.

CREAMY WHITE FROSTING

1	cup shortening
1$^1/_2$	teaspoons vanilla
$^1/_2$	teaspoon lemon extract, orange extract, or almond extract
4$^1/_2$	cups sifted powdered sugar
3	to 4 tablespoons milk

WHAT TO DO

1 Beat shortening, vanilla, and extract with an electric mixer on medium speed for 30 seconds. Gradually add half of the powdered sugar,

As dainty as fresh-picked blossoms, these candy flowers pose in pretty pastels against white frosting.

beating well. Add 2 tablespoons of the milk. Gradually beat in remaining powdered sugar and enough remaining milk to reach spreading consistency.

HOW TO DECORATE

1 Frost cupcakes with frosting. If desired, place some of the frosting in a decorating bag fitted with a star, rose, or round tip. Pipe desired frosting border on cupcakes.

2 Each gumdrop decoration uses two to four small gumdrops. To make any of the gumdrop decorations, on a surface sprinkled with sugar, roll out gumdrops to about 1/8-inch thickness. Keep gumdrops from sticking to rolling pin by sprinkling additional sugar on top of gumdrops while rolling.

3 For rosebud, roll out pink gumdrops and cut oval petals (about 1×3/4 inch). Roll up first petal like a jelly roll. Wrap second petal around first. Slightly curl top edge of petal out. Press a third petal around outside and curl the top edge out. Pinch off excess gumdrop at bottom of rose. Roll out green gumdrops and cut out leaf shapes using kitchen shears* or small leaf cutters. For tulip, roll out orange, yellow, pink, or purple gumdrops. Cut out teardrop shapes (about 1×3/4 inch) using kitchen shears. Lay first petal on work surface with point up. Layer two more petals on top with their points slightly turned out. Layer two more petals on top with their points even more turned out. Press all the petals together to stick. Roll out a green gumdrop and cut out slender leaves; arrange at bottom of tulip. For pansy, roll out purple and yellow gumdrops. (For a bicolored effect, roll out a colored gumdrop and a white gumdrop together, overlapping slightly.) Cut out 1-inch round petals. With fingers, pinch a pleat on one side of each petal. Place two yellow and two purple petals together. Arrange all four with pleats toward center. Pinch them all together. Position green leaves.

4 After shaping the decorations, press them into frosting on cupcakes. Freeze decorated cupcakes for up to two weeks before serving.

*Note: To keep kitchen shears, cutters, or knives from sticking, spray lightly with nonstick coating.

Talk With Your Kids
Talk about flowers that are edible.

Flowerpot Favors

Bright Idea
......
Tape a name card to a toothpick and poke it in the center of the favor for a place card.

SUPPLIES

Large plastic lids, such as those from laundry detergent, hair spray, or shaving cream; assorted ribbon and satin ribbon flowers
Scissors; strong adhesive, such as E6000

WHAT TO DO

1 Cut ribbons to fit around lid, covering as much of the lid as possible. Glue the ribbons on the lid using small dabs of adhesive.

2 Glue ribbon flowers on the mini flowerpots where desired. Let the adhesive dry.

RECYCLE PLASTIC LIDS INTO ELEGANT PARTY FAVORS USING A FEW SCRAPS OF TRIM.

MAKE IT A FAMILY TRADITION TO SERVE BIRTHDAY CAKE ON A SPECIAL STAND THAT'S BRIMMING WITH FESTIVE ACCENTS.

Talk With Your Kids

If they could celebrate their birthdays anywhere in the world, where would it be?

Party Cake Plate

SUPPLIES

Glass cake plate; enamel acrylic paints for painting on glass and ceramics
Assorted paintbrushes; pencil with good eraser

WHAT TO DO

1 Choose a cake plate that tolerates oven heat if baking is required to set the paint you are using. Some paints only require air drying. Begin with clean, dry cake plate. Plan design on plate. Avoid painting areas that contact food.

2 Paint in solid areas first, such as the scalloped edge on plate shown *above*. Let dry before painting other colors on top.

3 Make dots using the eraser of a pencil; dip in paint and dot onto surface. Let dry. Add smaller dots the same way using the handle of a paintbrush.

4 Paint in letters using different colors and personal style of lettering. Use a medium round or flat soft brush. Paint two coats of paint if needed for solid letters; let dry between coats.

5 Paint stripes, dots, or patterns of any kind on the letters in contrasting colors. Let dry.

257

Funky Fish Invitations

SUPPLIES

Tracing paper; pencil; scissors; solid and patterned scrapbook papers; glue stick; small hole punch
Flower-shape eyelets; eyelet tool; black marking pen
Purchased 6½×4¾-inch envelopes

WHAT TO DO

1 Enlarge and trace the fish pattern, *below*, onto tracing paper and cut it out. Trace around the shape on two scrapbook papers. Cut out the shapes.

2 Glue the fin onto the fish. Align the two paper layers. Punch a hole through both layers of the fish shapes where an eye is desired. Insert the eyelet into the holes; secure eyelet using the eyelet tool.

3 Use a marking pen to draw black details, referring to the photos, *left*, as a guide. Write the party information on the inside of the card.

4 Trim each envelope flap by gluing on a paper strip cut from scrapbook paper.

ATTACHED WITH AN EYELET, TWO PAPER LAYERS CUT INTO THE SHAPE OF A FISH ANNOUNCE AN OUTING IN STYLE.

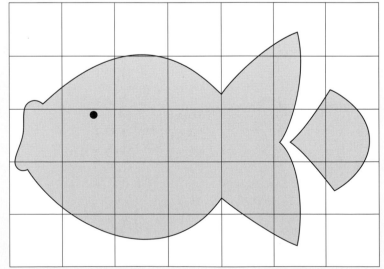

Funky Fish Invitations   **1 Square = 1 Inch**

258

Fish Charm Bracelets

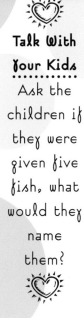

Talk With Your Kids

Ask the children if they were given five fish, what would they name them?

SUPPLIES

Silver color heavy chain bracelet; ruler
2 yards of ⅛-inch-wide yellow ribbon scissors; fish charms
Small piece of 24-gauge wire; 6 mm oval wire beads in red,
* purple, and fuchsia; silver-color spacers*

WHAT TO DO

1 Locate center link of bracelet. Cut a 6-inch-long piece of ribbon. Thread ribbon through hole in fish charm. Bend one end of wire over to form a small loop and twist, forming a wire needle. Thread both ribbon ends through eye of wire needle and pull through one wire bead. Thread ribbon ends through center link and knot ribbon in back. Thread ribbon ends back through wire beads. Cut off excess.

2 To attach side bead, cut one piece of ribbon 6 inches long. Count six links away from center link and thread ribbon through link. Thread ribbon through wire needle and use wire needle to thread ribbon ends through one wire bead and one spacer. Knot ribbon at the bottom and cut off excess. Repeat this process for other side bead.

SEND PARTY GUESTS HOME WITH FANCY FISH BRACELETS JANGLING ON THEIR WRISTS.

Bright Idea
Use this same shape for a television-theme cake.

Fishbowl Cake

SUPPLIES

  1 recipe Creamy White Frosting (see page 254–255)
     Liquid or paste food coloring in light blue and peach
  1 recipe White Confetti Cake
  1 cup small pebblelike candies, such as Nerds
  1 purchased tube of blue piping gel
     Decorating bag with medium rose tip and large star tip

WHITE CONFETTI CAKE

   2 cups all-purpose flour
   1 teaspoon baking powder
 $1/2$ teaspoon baking soda
 $1/8$ teaspoon salt
 $1/2$ cup shortening, butter, or margarine
$1^3/4$ cups sugar
   1 teaspoon vanilla
   4 egg whites
$1^1/3$ cups buttermilk or sour milk*
 $1/4$ cup multicolor nonpareils

1 Preheat oven to 350°. Grease and lightly flour two 8×1½-inch round baking pans; set pans aside. Stir together flour, baking powder, baking soda, and salt; set aside.

2 In a large mixing bowl beat shortening with an electric mixer on medium to high speed for 30 seconds. Add sugar and vanilla; beat until well combined. Add egg whites one at a time, beating well after each. Add flour mixture and buttermilk alternately to shortening mixture, beating on low speed after each addition just until combined. Stir in nonpareils. Pour batter into prepared pans.

3 Bake in preheated oven for 30 to 35 minutes or until a wood toothpick comes out clean. Cool cakes in pans on wire racks for 10 minutes. Remove cakes from pans; cool completely on racks.

Note: If buttermilk is unavailable, substitute sour milk in the same amount. For the 1⅓ cups of sour milk needed, place 1 tablespoon lemon juice or vinegar in a glass measuring cup. Add enough milk to make 1⅓ cups total liquid; stir. Let the mixture stand for 5 minutes before using it in a recipe.

HOW TO DECORATE

1 Set aside about ⅓ cup frosting for making fish. Tint the remaining frosting light blue using liquid or paste food coloring. Tint the ⅓ cup frosting peach.

2 Spread about ½ cup blue frosting on the bottom side of one of the cake rounds. Top with second cake round, placing it bottom side down. With a sharp serrated knife, remove a 1-inch slice from one side of cake. This makes a flat place for the bottom of fishbowl. Make another thin slice on opposite side of cake for top of fishbowl. Carefully stand up cake and place on serving plate. With a small metal spatula, spread blue frosting over cake. While frosting is still moist, press small pebblelike candies into frosting at bottom of cake.

3 Place the peach frosting in a decorating bag fitted with a medium rose tip. Pipe an oval shape for fish body. Make little ruffles for fish tail and fins. Place remaining blue frosting in a decorating bag fitted with a large star tip. Pipe a border at top of fishbowl. If desired, add a small round tip to pipe stripes on fish. Using blue piping gel, pipe bubbles above the fish. Cake serves 12.

SHAPED LIKE A FISHBOWL, THIS INGENIOUS CAKE IS SURE TO BRING GLEEFUL CHEERS. THE CANDIES AT THE BOTTOM GIVE COLOR AND TEXTURE BENEATH THE FROSTED FISH.

Talk With Your Kids
Talk about everyone's favorite dessert. Start a book to record those yummy recipes.

Bright Idea

Cut out colorful snowflakes and glue on the top of wrapped packages.

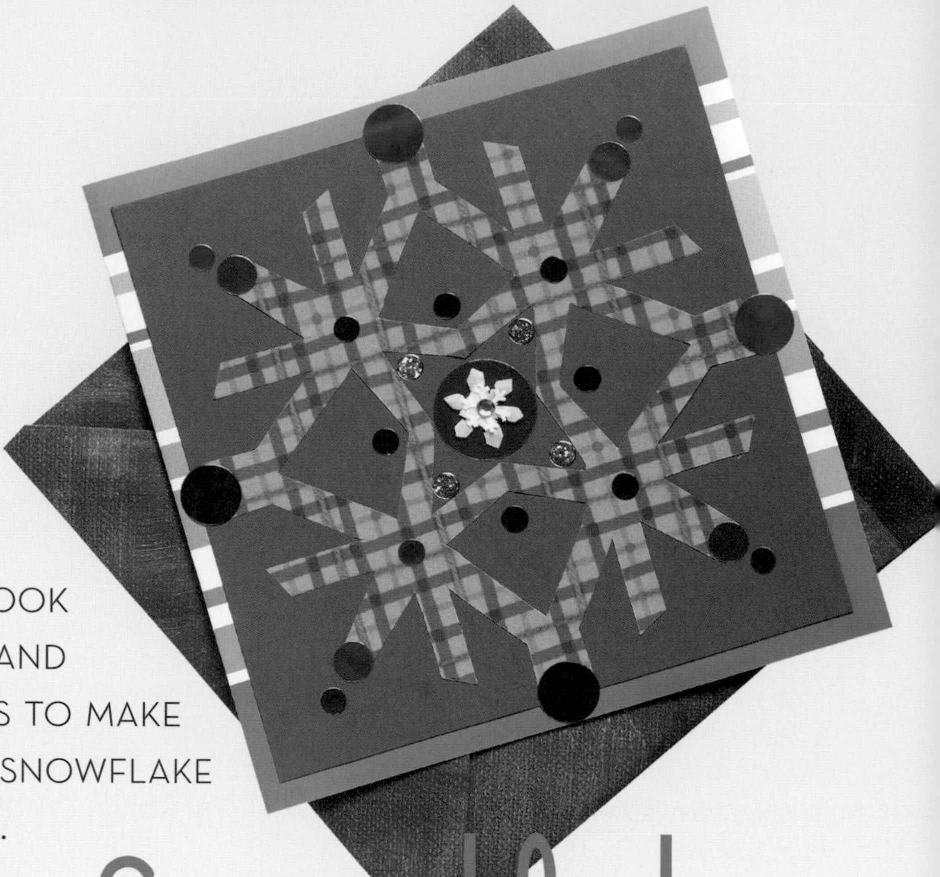

USE SCRAPBOOK PAPERS AND STICKERS TO MAKE FESTIVE SNOWFLAKE DESIGNS.

Snazzy Snowflake Invitations

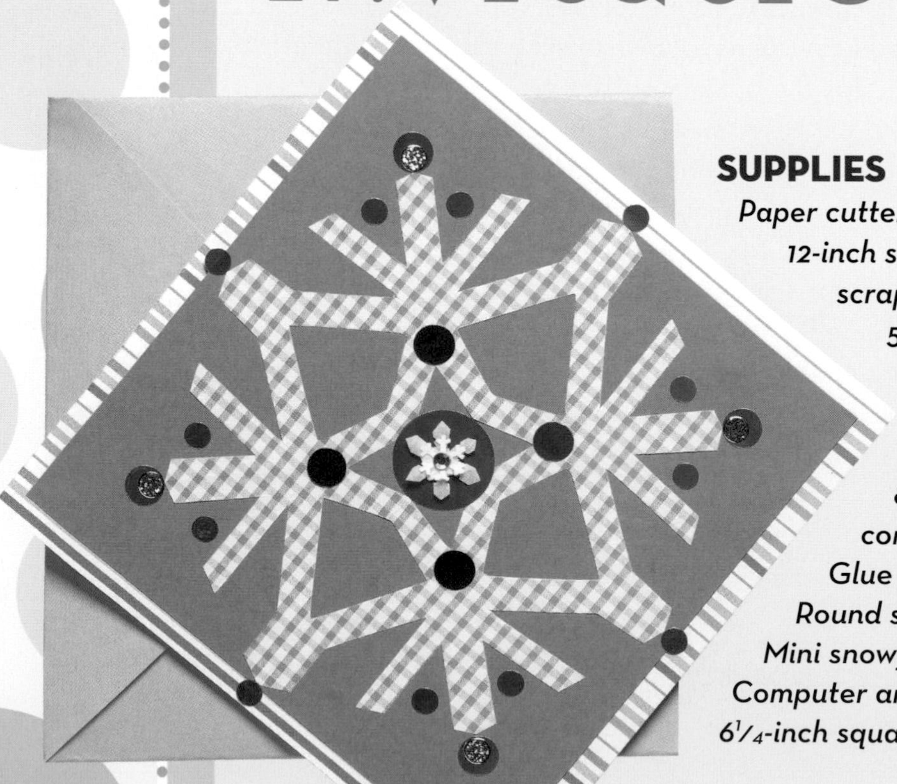

SUPPLIES

Paper cutter
12-inch squares of striped scrapbook paper
$5^1/_2$-inch squares of plaid scrapbook paper
Pencil
Scissors; ruler
$8^1/_2$×11-inch pieces of contrasting solid paper
Glue stick
Round stickers
Mini snowflake stickers
Computer and printer, optional
$6^1/_4$-inch square envelopes

WHAT TO DO

1. Use a paper cutter to cut the striped paper in half, cutting with the direction of the stripes. Fold short ends together to make a card.

2. Fold the plaid paper square in half. Fold in half again, aligning open corners together. Fold crosswise (points together) with folded edges together.

3. Trace a pattern, *below*, onto one side of the folded paper. Carefully cut along the lines. Unfold the snowflake.

4. Cut a 5½-inch square of solid paper. Glue the snowflake in the center. Glue to the front of the striped card. Press stickers on and around the snowflake as desired.

5. On a solid piece of paper, print or write the following to fit in a 5-inch square: Oh, the weather outside is frightful—
    But Saturday will be delightful!
    We'll have a party and some fun—
    Won't you come, won't you come, won't you come?

6. Cut out the invitation information in a 5-inch square. Glue to the inside of the card and embellish it with stickers.

7. Place each invitation in an envelope.

Talk With Your Kids
Talk about other ways to use paper snowflakes to decorate the house.

Snowflake Pattern

Alternate Snowflake Pattern

Alternate Snowflake Pattern

Alternate Snowflake Pattern

Alternate Snowflake Pattern

Alternate Snowflake Pattern

A GORGEOUS TREAT FOR ANY WINTER BIRTHDAY, THIS PRETTY CAKE IS BLANKETED IN FONDANT EMBELLISHED WITH COOKIE-CUTTER SNOWFLAKES.

Snowflake Cake

Bright Idea

Sprinkle each dessert plate with a pinch of edible glitter before serving.

SUPPLIES

- 1 recipe White Chocolate Cake
- 1 recipe Creamy White Frosting (see pages 254–255)
  Blue paste food coloring
- 1½ 24-ounce boxes prepared fondant (36 ounces total)
  Powdered sugar
  Assorted snowflake cookie cutters
  Clear edible glitter and/or sanding sugar

WHITE CHOCOLATE CAKE

- 4 egg whites
- 1¾ cups all-purpose flour
- 2 teaspoons baking powder
- ¼ teaspoon salt
- 3 ounces white chocolate baking bar, chopped
- ¾ cup half-and-half, light cream, or milk
- ⅓ cup butter or margarine
- 1 cup sugar
- 1½ teaspoons vanilla
- 4 egg yolks

1 In a bowl allow egg whites to stand at room temperature for 30 minutes. Meanwhile grease and lightly flour two 8×1½-inch round baking pans; set pans aside. Stir together flour, baking powder, and salt; set aside.

2 In a small heavy saucepan melt the chopped baking bar with ¼ cup of the half-and-half over very low heat, stirring constantly until baking bar starts to melt. Immediately remove from heat; stir until baking bar is completely melted and smooth. Stir in remaining half-and-half; cool.

3 Preheat oven to 350°. In a large mixing bowl beat the butter with an electric mixer on medium to high speed for 30 seconds. Add sugar and vanilla; beat until well combined. Add egg yolks one at a time, beating until combined. Add the flour mixture and baking bar mixture alternately to butter mixture, beating on low to medium speed after each addition just until combined.

4 Beat egg whites with a mixer on high speed until stiff peaks form (tips stand straight). Fold egg whites into the batter. Spread batter in pans.

5 Bake in preheated oven for 25 to 30 minutes or until a wooden toothpick comes out clean. Cool cakes in pans on wire racks for 10 minutes. Remove cakes from pans. Cool completely on racks.

HOW TO DECORATE

1 To assemble, place one cake layer on a cake plate. Frost cake layer with some of the frosting. Place the second cake layer and frost top and sides of cake. Mix a very small amount of blue paste food coloring with two-thirds of the fondant (24 ounces). Knead with your hands until color is uniform. Keep fondant wrapped with plastic until needed.

2 On a surface lightly dusted with powdered sugar, roll out the light blue fondant to about ¼-inch thickness in a circle about 14 inches in diameter. Sprinkle additional powdered sugar over rolled fondant to keep it from sticking to rolling pin. Gently loosen the underside of rolled fondant. Loosely roll fondant onto rolling pin. Transfer to top of cake. Lightly smooth and flatten fondant against the sides of cake, allowing excess fondant to gather at bottom of cake. With a smooth knife edge or metal spatula, trim excess fondant at bottom edge of cake.

3 On surface dusted with powdered sugar, roll out the remaining third of white fondant (12 ounces) to ⅛-inch thickness. Trim to an 11-inch circle. Make delicate snowflake cutouts in fondant using assorted snowflake cookie cutters. With a long metal spatula, gently loosen fondant from surface. With a pastry brush, lightly brush top of cake with water. Transfer snowflake fondant to top of cake as shown in photo, *above*. Lightly press to seal to cake top. If desired, use the cutout scraps to decorate bottom edge of cake. Use pastry brush to lightly brush backs of snowflake cutouts with water; stick to cake. To make cake top sparkle, sprinkle cake with clear edible glitter and/or sanding sugar. Cake serves 12.

Talk With Your Kids

Talk about why snowflakes always have six sides.

Bugs and Beetles Bash

"Can I Bug You?" Party Invitation

SUPPLIES

Foam brush; bristle art brush; acrylic paints in purple, magenta, orange, and lime; foam stamps in beetle and ladybug motifs
Card stock in black, violet, and white
Scissors, ruler, double-sided tape; computer; printer
⅛-inch hole punch; 2 silver brads

WHAT TO DO

1 Using the foam and bristle brushes, brush acrylic paints onto one foam stamp. Refer to the photo for color placement. Stamp the painted stamp on black card stock. Repeat for the other stamp. Let dry. Cut out shapes ⅛ inch from the edge.

2 Cut one 4¼×5½-inch rectangle from black card stock and one 4×5¼-inch rectangle from violet card stock. Tape the rectangles together.

3 Create the invitation text on a computer to fit a 3¾×5-inch rectangle, leaving spaces for the bugs. Print the invitation on white card stock. Cut out the invitation; tape it to the violet rectangle.

4 Punch a hole in the center bottom of each bug. Place the bugs on the invitation so they cover all of the words except the "Can I BUG you?" title. Punch a hole through the invitation rectangles; secure the bugs to the invitation with the silver brads.

TWO LITTLE PESTS SCUTTLE OVER THIS INVITATION. GUESTS HAVE TO SHOO THEM ASIDE TO READ IT!

Fluttery Flyaway Favor

SUPPLIES

Purple pencil; chenille stems in purple, lime, and black
Ruler; scissors; glitter card stock in green and purple
Thick white crafts glue; hole punch

WHAT TO DO

1 Wrap 2 inches of the eraser end of the pencil with a purple chenille stem. Trim off the extra.

2 Cut two small triangle wings from green glitter card stock.

3 Twist the center of the lime chenille stem ½ inch from the end of the eraser. Shape each tail to fit around the card stock triangles; cut off the extra. Glue the card stock triangles to each shaped chenille stem.

4 Cut a 4-inch piece of black chenille stem. Twist around eraser end and shape as antennae.

5 Punch four dots from purple card stock. Glue one dot on each wing and one on each antenna tip. Let dry.

6 Punch three dots from lime card stock. Glue dots in a row on the pencil below the bug.

continued on page 268

Talk With Your Kids

Discuss how moths live and how many species there are in the world.

Night Crawler Cake

SUPPLIES

Tracing paper; pencil; ruler; scissors; tape; cake mix (any flavor)
9×12-inch baking pan; knife; spatula; 28-inch-long platter
2 cans vanilla icing; food coloring in yellow and red
Candy-coated chocolate; red shoelace licorice
2 cinnamon-swirl shortbread cookies
Cherry sour candy; green licorice twist

WHAT TO DO

1 Draw two 4½×12-inch rectangles on tracing paper. Cut out the rectangles; tape short ends together into a long strip. Draw a wormlike shape on the paper. Remove the tape; use the two pieces for a pattern.

2 Prepare the cake mix and bake it in a 9×12-inch pan according to package directions. Let the cake cool; freeze it for easier shaping.

3 Remove the cake from the freezer. Run a knife around the edge and down the long center to loosen edges and to cut cake in half. Use the knife and spatula to work rectangles out of the pan.

4 Lay one pattern on top of one cake rectangle. Using a knife, carve around the pattern. Remove the pattern; carve out the shape.

UGH! WOULD YOU EAT A BUG? THIS ONE IS ESPECIALLY YUMMY, MADE FROM CAKE, COOKIES, AND CANDY.

Bright Idea
Make cupcakes and let kids decorate them however they wish.

Remove crumbs from top. Cut curved edges around the cake shape except along the short, straight end. Position this cake half on platter.

5 Repeat Step 4 for other cake rectangle. Place cakes together on platter, matching short ends.

6 Tint the icing orange by mixing red and yellow food colorings. Frost cake. Press candy-coated chocolate stripes across the top. Cut 2-inch lengths of red shoelace licorice for legs. Push legs into the cake.

7 Cut away bottom one-third of two cookies for eyes. Cut a cherry sour candy in half for irises. Use icing to hold irises to cookie eyes. Push eyes into cake. Position a candy-coated chocolate for the nose. Create a mouth from two ½-inch green licorice twist pieces. Cut six 2-inch lengths of shoelace licorice for the eyelashes. Push three lashes into the cake behind each eye.

"Glow Little Glowworm" Treat Cups

SUPPLIES

Tracing paper; pencil; scissors; tape
Two 9-ounce paper cups in contrasting colors

continued on page 270

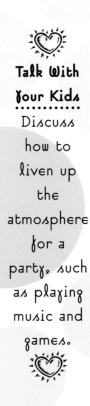

Talk With Your Kids

Discuss how to liven up the atmosphere for a party, such as playing music and games.

Bugs and Beetles Bash continued

Hole punches in ¹/₁₆- and ¹/₄-inch sizes; black plastic lace
Thick white crafts glue; wiggly eyes in round and oval assorted sizes
Black permanent marking pen

WHAT TO DO

1. Trace the pattern outline, *opposite*, onto tracing paper and cut out. Tape pattern around the cup to use on the outside. Trace the outline on the cup. Cut out the glowworm. Use both hole punches to punch out holes around the head and along the body bumps.

2. Cut a 4-inch length of plastic lace for the antennae; trim ends at an angle. Working from inside the cup, thread the lace ends through two punched holes in the head.

3. Glue mismatched eyes below the antennae. Use the marking pen to draw a small nose and wide smile. Outline the bottom edge of the body. Slip the second cup inside the finished glowworm cup.

Bug Bits Trail Mix

SUPPLIES

- 1 10-ounce bag cheddar-cheese-flavor sourdough hard pretzel pieces
- 1 2⁵/₈-ounce container mini tortilla chips
- 1 2¹/₂-ounce container mini cheese-flavor crispy puffed snacks
- 1 9-ounce box raisins
- 3 1.7-ounce cans shoestring potato sticks
- 1 3-ounce package hickory-smoke beef jerky, torn into small pieces
- 1 9-ounce bag natural blue corn tortilla chips

WHAT TO DO

1. Mix the first six ingredients in a large serving bowl. Gently mix in blue corn chips.

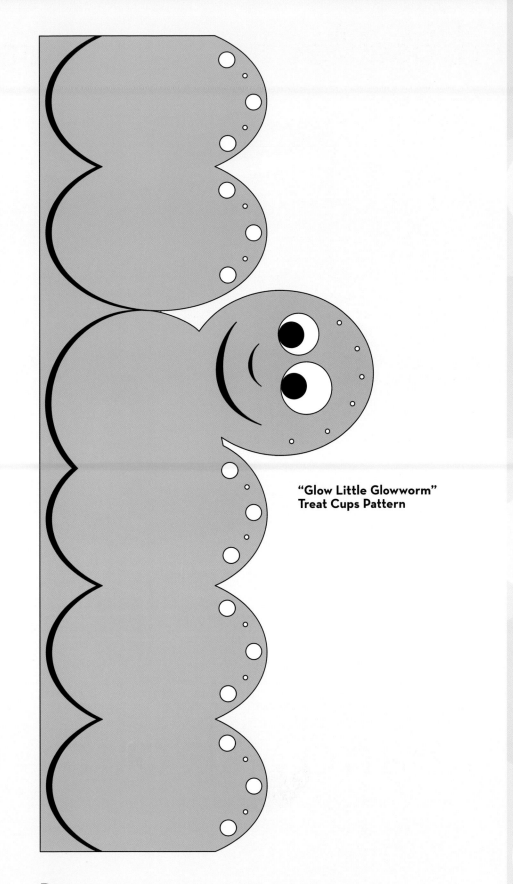

**"Glow Little Glowworm"
Treat Cups Pattern**

**Talk With
Your Kids**
Talk about
how
caterpillars
turn into
butterflies
and what
they look
like at
various
stages.

DRESS TREAT CUPS IN GLOWWORM
"COSTUMES" AND FILL THEM WITH CRUNCHY
BUG BITS (A TASTY TRAIL MIX).

CHAPTER
8

Out and About

This chapter is packed with family-fun ideas—
travel games, scrapbook pages, clever suitcases—
to make even more vacation memories!

Bright
Idea
• • • • •
Keep a
plastic
storage
box in the
car and
pack it
with travel
games.

Fun and Games Travel Book

"Travel Fun and Games" Book Cover

SUPPLIES

3-ring binder; tracing paper; pencil; ruler; fabric shears
Felt yardage in dark blue, orange, lime, gold, and light blue
Fast-drying fabric glue, such as Beacon Fabri-Tac, or thick white crafts glue
Pinking shears; 1 yard of orange ribbon; scissors

WHAT TO DO

1 Open the binder flat on tracing paper. Draw around the binder; add
¼ inch to all edges. This is the cover pattern. Cut two covers from felt,

SOME BOOKS ARE MEANT FOR READING. THIS ONE'S FOR PLAY!

one dark blue (outer) and one orange (inner). Glue the dark blue cover on top of a piece of lime felt, allowing at least 1/4 inch of felt all around. Use pinking shears to cut out the cover, leaving a 1/8-inch lime border.

2 Measure the width of the binder's spine; cut away (and discard) this measurement from the center of the orange cover. The two pieces left are the inner covers.

3 Cut the ribbon in half. Center and glue one end of each ribbon to the lime side of outer cover.

4 Glue each orange inner cover to the lime side of the outer cover at the top, bottom, and ribboned edges, creating pockets where you will insert the binder.

5 To cover around the metal rings, cut a piece of lime felt the height of binder plus 1/2 inch each to the width and height. Cut the piece in half lengthwise. Tuck and glue each half behind the rings, wrapping 1/4 inch of the felt at the top and bottom around binder.

6 Slip the binder flaps into the pockets. Lay the binder open. Glue the pocket openings closed.

7 Trace the patterns on pages 278–279 onto tracing paper. Cut out the patterns from felt scraps. Also cut out assorted shapes, such as squares and rectangles for buildings and ovals and long squiggles for bodies of water. Decorate the binder cover and add small pockets to the inner covers, referring to the photos for ideas. Glue the pieces in place.

Let's Play Checkers!

SUPPLIES

Metal-cutting scissors; 30-gauge galvanized flat sheet metal (available in the air duct section of home supply stores) Ruler; hammer, large nail; three 1/2-inch eyelets

continued on page 276

Fun and Games Travel Book continued

Bright

Idea

·····

Cut postcard-size pieces of card stock and let the kids color and send them when on vacation.

Spray adhesive 3-ring binder; notebook paper
Felt in orange, gold, light blue, and dark blue
Fabric shears; pinking shears; fast-drying fabric glue
Twenty-four ½-inch-diameter ceramic magnets
Acrylic paints in white, lime, and orange
Paintbrush; clear acrylic spray; ruler; three-hole punched notebook paper

WHAT TO DO

1 Cut a $9\frac{3}{8}$×10-inch piece of sheet metal. Round the corners to match your binder. Using the notebook paper, mark three holes on one 10-inch side, placing the center hole 5 inches from the top.

2 Using a hammer and a nail, punch the three holes wide enough for the eyelet to fit freely. Hammer smooth any rough edges on the holes. Recheck fit.

3 Spray adhesive over one side of the metal; place, glue side down, on the orange felt. Trim around the edges with scissors. Spray the opposite side with adhesive. Place on gold felt. Use pinking shears to trim ⅛ inch from the edge. Add eyelets to the holes, following the package directions.

4 For the game board, cut thirty-two 1-inch felt squares (16 light blue and 16 dark blue). Use fabric glue to affix the squares, alternating colors, into a larger 8-inch square in the center on the orange side.

5 For playing pieces, clean the magnets. Base-coat the magnets white, placing them on a metal strip to make painting easier. Paint 12 of the magnets lime and 12 orange. Paint several coats, allowing drying time between the coats. Finish with several coats of clear acrylic spray. Let the magnets dry 24 hours.

It's a Go for Tic-Tac-Toe!

Notes: The materials are the same as those listed for the checkers game, with the following changes: You use only three colors of felt (dark blue, gold, and lime), and you need only eight ceramic magnets for playing pieces.

Create tic-tac-toe and checkers games on separate boards or on the front and back of the same board. For a separate board, use dark blue and gold felt. Follow steps 1 through 3 for the checkers game.

WHAT TO DO

1 Cut four 1×10-inch strips of lime felt. Create the grid with the strips; use fabric glue to adhere in place. Follow Step 5 of checkers to make playing pieces.

Write a Silly Sentence

SUPPLIES
Magazines; scissors; glue stick; white card stock
Spray adhesive; felt in desired color
3-ring zippered pencil pouch

WHAT TO DO

1 Cut out words and pictures from magazines. Be sure to include words for all parts of a sentence. Glue the pieces to card stock. Apply spray adhesive to the back of the card stock; press on felt. Cut out the words and pictures. Store pieces in the pouch.

2 To play, select 10 pieces from the pouch. Assign a specific amount of time for making a sentence. Award a point for each piece used. The first person to reach a certain number of points wins.

Create a Felt Picture

SUPPLIES
Tracing paper; pencil; fabric shears; felt in assorted colors
3-ring zippered pencil pouch

WHAT TO DO

1 Trace patterns on *pages 278–279* onto tracing paper; cut patterns from felt. Store pieces in the pouch. Use the felt pieces to make a picture on the back of the binder.

Talk With Your Kids

Talk about ways to be a good sport when playing any kind of game.

Travel Fun

**Fun and Games
Travel Book Patterns**

**Fun and Games
Travel Book Patterns**

SUPPLIES

Newspapers
Masking tape
Small, hard-surface suitcase
Bright pink spray paint
Purple enamel paint; paintbrush
Permanent black marking pen
Scissors
1-inch-wide purple grosgrain ribbon
Strong adhesive, such as E6000
Tracing paper; pencil
Scrapbook papers in various prints
Decoupage medium
Circle cutter or lids in various sizes
Buttons

Let's Go Tote

WHAT TO DO

1 In a well-ventilated work area, cover the work surface with newspapers.

2 Cover the metal hardware on the suitcase with masking tape to protect it from being painted. Place the suitcase on the newspapers.

3 Spray-paint the suitcase and let it dry. Apply a second coat if necessary and let dry. Paint the top of the lid purple; let dry.

4 Use the marking pen to write "Let's go!" around the sides of the suitcase lid.

5 Cut a piece of ribbon to fit around the suitcase. With the ends in the back, use strong adhesive to glue the piece of ribbon on the suitcase. Let dry.

6 Trace the shirt pattern, *opposite*. Cut out the shape. Trace around the shirt pattern on scrapbook papers to make approximately eight shirts. Fold back the collars and glue in place with decoupage medium.

7 Arrange and glue the shirts around the suitcase using decoupage medium to glue them onto the ribbon and suitcase.

8 Using a circle cutter (or tracing lids and cutting with scissors), cut out several sizes of circles from scrapbook papers. Trim some of the circles to fit along the edge of the suitcase lid. Arrange the circles and glue them in place using decoupage medium.

9 Use strong adhesive to glue small buttons on the shirts and large and small buttons on some of the lid circles. Let dry.

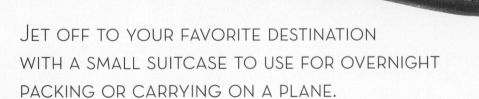

Jet off to your favorite destination with a small suitcase to use for overnight packing or carrying on a plane.

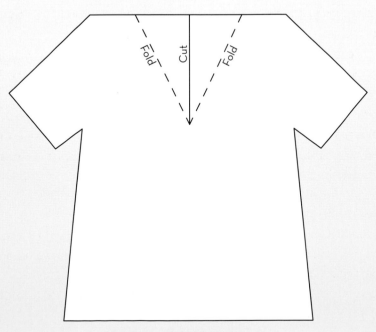

Let's Go Tote Shirt Pattern

Talk With Your Kids

Discuss a checklist of items the kids need for travel, then let them pack their bags, checking the list as they go.

Bright Idea
......
Photocopy your scrapbook pages to share with other family members for their books.

Our Reunion

Combine ready-made items to make a clever scrapbook page:
- Recycle old maps and atlases to embellish the background.
- Cut a hill from contrasting card stock.
- Use fabric appliqué cars to add colorful details.
- Create flower and dot accents with foam stickers.
- Use foam alphabet stickers to make a dimensional headline.
- Make a journal box using computer type.

COMBINE RECYCLED MATERIALS AND NEW DETAILS TO MAKE A TRAVEL PAGE THAT'S PACKED WITH PIZZAZZ.

A GLORIOUS DAY AT THE BEACH, AQUA-BLUE WATER, SPARKLING WHITE SAND, AND WARM SUNSHINE INSPIRED THESE CAREFREE SUMMER PAGES.

Sand Castles

Keep your beach vacation memories fresh using these tips for a sparkling page:

- Use small seashells to add dimension.
- Choose a watercolor background paper with smooth, warm or cool blended colors to carry out the beach theme.
- Use several face sizes to provide interest and variety.
- Retrace the journaling with a glue pen and sprinkle it with glitter.
- Arrange photos with the direction of the faces looking outward or toward the center of the spreads.
- Crop some photos as silhouettes.

Talk With Your Kids
Discuss each family member's favorite thing to do while traveling.

WITH A COLOR-BLOCK
BACKGROUND, YOU
CAN MAKE THESE
PAGES QUICKER
THAN YOU CAN SAY,
"LET'S HIKE!"

Keep it simple
to make these
photo-rich pages:
- Color-block the
  background for
  instant interest.
- Crop all photos
  approximately
  the same size.
- Trim the page
  with fibers.
- Mat one photo
  for a focal
  point.
- Print headline
  and journal box on vellum and attach with eyelets.

Camping at Thomas Mitchell Park

Glossary

ACRYLIC PAINT—A water-based, quick-drying paint that cleans up with soap and water. Some are developed for outdoor use while others are for interior use only.

CARD STOCK—Heavy solid-color paper available in large sheets in art stores and small sheets in scrapbooking stores.

CHENILLE STEM—A velvety covered wire (pipe cleaner) that can be purchased in a variety of sizes and colors, including metallic. Some chenille stems are striped.

CRAFTS FOAM—This foam is available in sheets of varying weight and many colors. It can also be purchased in precut shapes and letters.

DECOUPAGE—The technique of cutting out designs (usually from paper) and mounting them on a surface using decoupage medium or a half-and-half mixture of glue and water.

DISPOSABLE—Something meant to be used once and then thrown away.

DOWEL—A solid square or round cylinder of wood that comes in many sizes.

FRAY—To pull away the threads at the edge of fabric.

GEMS—In crafting terms, a plastic rhinestone or smooth colorful stone that is backed with metallic silver to make it sparkle.

GLASS PAINTS—These paints can be acrylic (water-based) or enamel (oil-based). Some glass paints require the painted object to be baked in the oven for the paint to become permanent.

IRIDESCENT—Showing changes in color when seen from different angles.

KNEAD—To mix by pressing and squeezing materials, such as clay, together.

POLYMER CLAY—An easy-to-mold clay that becomes hard and permanently shaped when baked in the oven. Common brands are Sculpey, Fimo, and Premo.

PONY BEADS—Colorful plastic beads (round and shapes), ranging from about the size of a pea to the size of a nickel, with a large hole in the center.

RUBBER STAMPS—A block, usually wood, that has a rubber design on one side. To stamp, the rubber surface is pressed onto an ink pad, then pressed on a surface to transfer the design.

SCRAPBOOK PAPERS—Solid, print, and textured papers created specifically for scrapbooking and cardmaking. Common sizes are 12-inch squares and 8½×11 inches.

SEED BEADS—Small round glass beads often used in jewelry making. The beads are available in a variety of sizes and colors.

TRACING—Drawing around an object or copying the lines of drawn art.

TRACING PAPER—A thin sheet of semi-transparent paper used to trace drawings or patterns.

WAXED PAPER—Available in rolls, this paper has a moisture-proof coating and is often used to cover a work surface when crafting.

Index

Bright Idea

Photocopy the patterns and keep them handy in a large envelope.

continued on page 288

Talk With Your Kids
Take turns telling what type of artwork you each like best, including techniques, styles, and colors.

Index continued

Bright Idea

Create a crafts zone where projects in the works can sit.